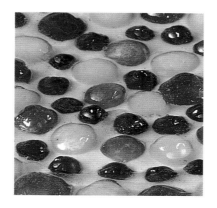

100 GREAT FRUIT DESSERTS

ABIGAIL JOHNSON DODGE

PHOTOGRAPHS BY
ROBIN MATTHEWS

WEIDENFELD
& NICOLSON
LONDON

CONTENTS

5

Introduction

7

Storecupboard

9

Helpful Hints for Choosing Fruit

11

Selecting Ripe Fruit

13

The Recipes

Pies, Cakes, Tarts; Puddings, Custards, Teatime Treats; Mousses,
Soufflés, Sabayons; Ice Creams, Sorbets, Granitas; Fresh Fruits
and Compôtes

58

Basics

62

Recipe Index

INTRODUCTION

In my opinion, there is nothing more glamorous, satisfying and delicious than a fruit dessert. A tender, ripe fruit is just next to perfect and when that fruit is teamed with some of nature's other marvels, it is magnificent! In *100 Great Fruit Desserts* some of nature's best combinations will rise up out of the kitchen with little effort from you and yet outstanding results. You, your family, friends and guests will be awestruck by glorious desserts that in most cases are super easy and quick to prepare.

Fruit desserts have the added benefit of being remarkably low in fat – and high in vitamins, too! Nature has already loaded many fruits with flavour, sweetness and texture so any additional ingredients need not be excessively sugary or fatty. Fruit desserts can stand on their own without hiding behind competitive flavours. In fact, a squeeze of lime and some chopped mint are all the Melon Compôte (see page 52) needs to bring out the best in the fruit's flavour. Only nature's most flavoursome citrus and a few strawberries are needed for the Citrus Terrine (see page 54) – a true show-stopper and a cinch to prepare)!

Of course, a bit of cream, butter and sugar added to a dessert heightens the flavour and enjoyment. But a small amount is usually all that's needed to emphasize the fruit's natural attributes. Imagine tarts glistening with glaze-topped berries or fruity ice creams that capitalize on summer's best market choices. Lemon-flavoured Virginia Sponge (see page 24) with macerated mixed berries or Classic Cherry Clafouti (see page 32) are tempting and delicious without being unnecessarily laden with fat and calories.

100 Great Fruit Desserts concentrates on recipes that maximize fruit flavour, please a variety of palates and are prepared with a minimum of difficulty. Whether serving yourself, your family or dinner guests, I hope you enjoy these versatile, refreshing fruit recipes as much as I do!

STORECUPBOARD

A well-stocked storecupboard is inspiration to any chef. Most items are readily available at the local supermarket but do frequent your local delicatessen or speciality shop for unusual ingredients. Although dry goods are easily forgotten at the back of a shelf, be sure to keep stocks fresh and always respect the use-by dates.

FLOUR

There are many varieties but types are definitely not interchangeable. Be sure to use the flour recommended in the recipe and to measure and weigh correctly as inaccuracies lead to disasters. If a recipe calls for sifting, then it is important to follow this as the measurements and final results are based on sifted quantities. All flour should be stored in airtight containers in a cool, dark place. The freezer or refrigerator is ideal for flours that are used infrequently. Discard any flour that has gone past its use-by date, or has become infested with bugs.

SPICES

Most baking spices like nutmeg, cinnamon, cloves, ginger or allspice are available whole or ground. For better flavour, it is always preferable to buy the spice whole and grind as needed using a small spice grinder (a small electric coffee grinder is perfect) or a grater, but nothing beats the convenience of ground spices in jars. Whatever option you choose, keep spices in a cool, dark place and be sure to dust the jars regularly.

FLAVOURINGS

Vanilla is the most popular and versatile of essences. It is available in liquid form, or in its original pod. Lemon, orange and coffee extracts are also available. Whatever you choose, be sure that it is not an imitation essence. Brandies, eau-de-vie and other liqueurs are also wonderful as dessert flavourings, sprinkled on sparingly as required, or whenever the fancy takes you, even if the recipe doesn't specify.

CHOCOLATE

This is available in many forms and is universally craved. I am never without a supply of unsweetened cocoa powder and a bar or two of plain and white chocolate.

SWEETENERS

Much like flours, sugars are not interchangeable and the type specified in the ingredients list of a recipe must be respected or the results may not be what you expected! The differing types all have varying degrees of coarseness and sweetness – some are more refined than others and some are flavoured with molasses. Icing sugar is very finely ground sugar mixed with cornflour and it must always be sifted before using. Brown sugars owe their taste, colour and sticky texture to the addition of molasses. The colour is an indication of the amount of molasses that has been used, with light sugars being the most lightly flavoured. All sugars must be stored in airtight containers in a cool, dark place. Honey is one of nature's purest sweeteners and its flavour and appearance depend upon the flowers from which it came. Keep the jar clean by wiping the rim after each use before recapping and keep in a cool, dark place. Do not refrigerate honey or it will crystallize.

DECORATIONS

Fruit is often beautiful enough to be a decoration in its own right, but it never hurts to keep a stock of baking decorations on hand. Coloured sugars, candied fruits and candied violets will all last a long time when stored tightly sealed and will be there to add a festive touch to a special occasion. Preserves like redcurrant jelly or apricot are essential for adding a shiny glaze to the tops of fruit tarts. Fresh herbs, such as mint, also make stunning decorations but these cannot be stored much longer than 2-3 days in the fridge.

DRIED FRUIT

Apricots, dates, figs, prunes and raisins are very useful storecupoboard items as their shelf-life is longer than fresh and their uses plentiful. Always choose brightly coloured, plump and moist fruit and keep in airtight containers for up to four months.

HELPFUL HINTS FOR CHOOSING FRUIT

The following is a guide to choosing, ripening and handling the most commonly available fruit. Appearance is the most obvious guideline, but bright shiny fruit are not always the best and most sweet tasting. It is also important to consider storage time as some fruits have longer keeping abilities than others.

APPLES

Selection: Many varieties are available so choose according to your needs. The fruit should be firm and bright in colour without bruises, blemishes or broken skin. It should smell fresh and never musty.

Ripening and Storage: If not using within 1 or 2 days, keep the fuit crisp in the fridge.

Handling: Rinse, peel, core and slice or follow recipe directions. Rub peeled fruit with lemon to prevent discoloration.

STONE FRUITS *(apricots, plums, peaches, nectarines)*

Selection: Choose plump, firm but not hard, brightly coloured fruit. The fruit's fragrance should be strong.

Ripening and Storage: Ripen at room temperature until just soft at shoulders. Use quickly or refrigerate to slow up the ripening.

Handling: Rinse, halve and discard stone. To peel, drop in boiling water for 10 seconds, then immerse in ice water and slip off skin.

BANANAS *(common variety)*

Selection: Yellow to greenish-yellow, firm unblemished bananas are best for eating or slicing. Choose unbruised fruit that are firmly attached to the stem.

Ripening and Storage: Ripen at room temperature. Yellow bananas with a few black spots are good for slicing. The blacker the banana is the riper and better for batters or baking in breads. Very ripe bananas can be frozen, in their skins, and used in batter recipes at a latter date.

Handling: Peel and slice, or mash.

BERRIES *(strawberries, blueberries, blackberries, currants, gooseberries, cranberries)*

Selection: Choose plump, even-coloured berries with no wrinkles and showing no signs of mould or moisture.

Ripening and Storage: Berries do not ripen once picked. Keep them refrigerated and use as soon as possible as they deteriorate quickly.

Handling: Rinse berries just before using. Drain them well and gently remove stems and caps.

CHERRIES

Selection: Look for large, well-coloured sweet cherries. The bigger and more fragrant they are the sweeter they will be. Bypass cherries that are soft, wrinkly or wet looking.

Ripening and Storage: Cherries are extremely perishable. Keep them refrigerated and use quickly.

Handling: Rinse cherries just before using. Drain them well and gently remove stems; de-stone them if necessary.

CITRUS *(lemons, limes, oranges, grapefruit)*

Selection: Choose firm, heavy, fragrant fruit. The fruit's colour should be bright and the skin without bruises.

Ripening and Storage: Citrus fruits are harvested fully ripe and should be kept refrigerated until use.

Handling: Use a box grater for zest and squeeze fruits for juice. For sections, cut away the rind and pith from stem to bottom. Cut along the membrane divisions to release the fruit segments. A small serrated knife is useful when preparing citrus fruit.

Above: Blueberry Queen of Puddings (see page 36)

GRAPES

Selection: Choose plump, well-coloured grapes firmly attached to the stem. Avoid wrinkled or washed-out grapes.

Ripening and Storage: Grapes do not ripen once picked. Keep them refrigerated loose in a plastic bag. Rinse and dry the grapes just before using.

KIWI FRUIT

Selection: Choose plump, firm but not hard fruit. The brown skin should be even coloured with no bruises.

Ripening and Storage: Ripen at room temperature until soft like a peach. Use them quickly or keep in the fridge until use.

Handling: Always peel away the brown skin before preparing the fruit according to recipe directions.

MANGOES

Selection: Choose plump, fragrant, unbruised fruit. The fruit should be firm yet slightly soft at the shoulders.

Ripening and Storage: Ripen mangoes at room temperature until they are redder or more yellow, depending on the variety. Use them quickly or store in the fridge for 2 days at most.

Handling: Slice off the skin and flesh together along both sides of the stone. Score the flesh in slices or squares and then invert the skin. Now cut chunks or slices of the flesh away from the skin. See the relevant recipes for other directions.

MELONS

Selection: Many varieties are available. Buy whole, uncut melons that are evenly coloured and heavier than they appear. Ripe melons should 'give' slightly by the shoulder and be very fragrant.

Ripening and Storage: Only whole melons will continue to ripen. Keep them at at room temperature until fully ripe before using immediately or refrigerate in a tightly sealed bag.

Handling: Cut the melon in half, then scoop out and discard the seeds before following recipe directions.

PAPAYAS

Selection: Choose slightly soft, fragrant fruit. It should appear more yellow than green.

Ripening and Storage: Ripen papayas at room temperature until yellow and soft but not mushy.

Handling: Cut the fruit in half, scoop out and discard seeds. The fruit can also be peeled and sliced.

PASSION FRUIT

Selection: Choose wrinkly, slightly shrivelled fruit.

Ripening and Storage: Ripen the fruit at room temperature until wrinkly. Use them quickly or refrigerate for about 2 or 3 days before using.

Handling: Cut the fruit in half and scoop out the pulp. Follow the recipe directions concerning straining.

PEARS

Selection: Many varieties are available. Choose the type suitable to your baking needs. The fruit should be slightly soft at the shoulders and well coloured without bruises, blemishes or broken skin. It should smell fragrant and never musty.

Ripening and Storage: Ripen pears at room temperature and use them quickly or refrigerate until ready to use.

Handling: See Apples.

PINEAPPLES

Selection: Choose a plump, brightly coloured fruit with a deep fragrance – no bruises or soft spots.

Ripening and Storage: Pineapples will not sweeten once picked, although they may get juicier. Keep them at room temperature and use within 1 or 2 days. Refrigerate cut pineapple.

Handling: Cut off the top and base. Slice away the rind from top to bottom. Proceed according to recipe directions.

RHUBARB

Selection: Choose firm, well-coloured stalks.

Ripening and Storage: Rhubarb will not ripen once picked. Keep it in the fridge, unwashed, for 3 or 4 days or freeze up to 3 months.

Handling: Cut away and discard the tops and bottoms of stalks. Rinse well and proceed with the recipe.

SELECTING RIPE FRUIT

The first step towards successful fruit desserts is the choice of top-quality ingredients. Fresh, flavoursome fruit is vital for a good end result and looks are not always an indication of taste.

It used to be that every fruit had a season and if you missed that special time of year you were out of luck. Technological advances have altered the concept of seasonal fruit; no longer are fruits bound by their local time slot with many available all year round. Cold storage allows us to enjoy delicious, crisp apples in June. Air freight sends us kiwi fruit from New Zealand in January and strawberries from South America in December. Indeed, air travel has allowed exotic fruits like mangoes, papayas and carambolas to be more accessible in the shops and hence more popular. While this is exciting and very enticing, it is more important than ever to choose your fruit carefully. Fruit buyers beware: just because it's available and looks pretty, it does not mean all fruit is delicious!

Become an educated consumer and know your fruit. All fruits have distinct characteristics for selection (see pages 9 and 10 for brief descriptions). Rely on your instincts to select ripe, sweet, delicious fruit every time. Smell, See, and Touch – SST for short – the fruit to assess its desirability. All three senses must work together to deliver perfect fruit to your kitchen. Smell the fruit: does it smell fragrant, ripe and good enough to eat? Touch the fruit: will it continue to ripen at home, does it feel firm, does it give slightly to pressure around the shoulders, is it heavier than it appears? How does the fruit look: is it correctly coloured, are there any blemishes or bruises, is the skin smooth and satiny? Before you shop, know the answers to these questions in order to select the best fruit available.

Lastly, developing a relationship with your greengrocer is a sure way to land the perfect fruit every time. She will aid your fruit selection depending on your recipe needs.

THE RECIPES

PIES, CAKES, TARTS

There is nothing more appealing than the smell of baked fruit mingling with butter, sugar and spices wafting throught the house. The following recipes offer a wealth of yummy smelling – and tasting – desserts. If you are unsure when it comes to handling pastry, see the tips on page 61 before you begin.

LINZERTORTE

When the dead of winter comes, remember 350g/12oz raspberry jam can be substituted for the fresh berries. Use a piping bag to pipe the lattice work and rim of the torte.

185g/6½ oz plain flour
90g/3½oz ground blanched hazelnuts or almonds
¾ tsp ground cinnamon
½ tsp ground cloves
1½ tbsp cocoa powder
175g/6 oz unsalted butter, at room temperature

200g/7oz granulated sugar
¼ tsp salt
1 egg, size 3
1 egg yolk, size 3
150g/5oz fresh raspberries tossed in 25g/1oz plain flour

Grease and line the bottom of 23cm/9in springclip baking tin. Sift together the flour, ground nuts, cinnamon, cloves and cocoa and set aside.

In a separate bowl, beat together the butter, sugar and salt until light and fluffy. Add the egg and egg yolk and beat until well blended. Stir in the flour mixture until just blended.

Press and spread about two-thirds of the mixture into the base of the baking tin. Spoon the raspberries (or raspberry jam) on to the mixture, keeping about 2.5cm/1in from the rim. Pipe the remaining mixture lattice-style or spoon it round the edge of the pan and on to the berries. Freeze for about one hour until firm.

Meanwhile, preheat the oven to 160°C/325°F/Gas 3.

Place the Linzertorte in the centre of the oven and bake for 55-60 minutes until the crust is firm and the berries are bubbling. Allow to cool completely before removing the tin and peeling off the lining paper.

RASPBERRY-CHOCOLATE TILE CAKE

Whether or not you glaze the cake with the ganache, make sure to serve it with a pool of red berry coulis.

350g/12oz dark chocolate, chopped
½ tsp instant coffee granules
65ml/2½fl oz hot water
100g/4oz unsalted butter, at room temperature

150g/5oz granulated sugar
6 eggs, size 3, separated
100g/4oz cake flour, sifted
150g/5oz raspberries

Preheat the oven to 180°C/350°F/Gas 4. Line a 900g/2 lb loaf tin that measures 23 x 12.5cm/9 x 5 in with foil, then grease it.

Melt the chocolate with the coffee and water, then allow to cool slightly. Meanwhile, beat the butter with all but 50g/2oz of the sugar until light and fluffy. Beat in the egg yolks one at a time. Stir in the chocolate mixture and fold in the flour until just incorporated.

Beat the egg whites until soft peaks form, add the remaining sugar and continue beating until glossy. Fold the whites and raspberries into the chocolate mixture. Pour the mixture into the prepared tin. Bake in a water bath placed in the centre of the oven for 70 minutes. Allow the cake to cool completely in the tin.

Trim off the top crust to level the cake and then refrigerate it overnight. Invert the cake on to a serving plate and remove the foil.

Keep the cake chilled until serving. Slice with a hot knife.

GANACHE GLAZE VARIATION:
Heat 175ml/6fl oz double cream until boiling. Stir in 175g/6oz chopped dark chocolate until smooth. Cool the mixture until warm.

Set the chilled cake on a rack set over a plate. Pour the ganache over the cake to evenly cover it. Use a palette knife to cover any holes in the sides. Refrigerate the cake until the glaze is set and ready to serve.

APRICOT UPSIDE-DOWN GINGERBREAD

A take-off of the classic upside-down cake that is sure to please. Ripe, flavoursome apricots will glaze whilst baking underneath the spicy cake. And a dollop of whipped cream when serving won't hurt!

FOR THE CARAMEL:
150g/5oz soft brown sugar
50ml/2fl oz water

FOR THE GINGERBREAD:
3 ripe apricots, stoned and sliced
270g/9½oz plain flour
4 tsp baking powder
1 tsp ground ginger
½ tsp ground cinnamon
½ tsp ground nutmeg
¼ tsp salt
100g/4oz unsalted butter, at room temperature
100g/4oz soft brown sugar
120g/4½oz molasses
1 egg, size 3
120ml/4fl oz buttermilk

Preheat the oven to 180°C/350°F/Gas 4. To make the caramel, see the technique in Coconut Crème Caramel (see page 41). Pour the caramel into a 20cm/8in square baking tin. Allow it to sit for 2 minutes before arranging the apricot slices on top. Set aside.

Sift together flour, baking powder, ginger, cinnamon, nutmeg and salt. In a separate bowl, beat together the butter and sugar until light and fluffy. Add the molasses and egg, beating to combine. Alternately stir the dry ingredients and the buttermilk into the butter and sugar mixture. Pour the mixture into the baking tin.

Bake in the centre of the oven for 45-50 minutes, or until a skewer inserted in the centre comes out clean. Remove from the oven and immediately invert the tin on to a serving plate. Allow it to sit for a few minutes before removing the gingerbread from the tin. Serve warm or at room temperature.

RASPBERRY GANACHE TART

Crisp pastry, a rich filling and tart raspberries make this dessert a real winner.

175ml/6fl oz double cream
175g/6oz dark chocolate, chopped
1 quantity Sweet Tart Pastry, baked blind in a 23cm/9in tart tin
275g/10oz raspberries
100g/4oz seedless raspberry jam, melted (optional)

Bring the cream to the boil, then remove it from the heat. Add the chocolate and stir until smooth. Pour the mixture into the prepared tart case and refrigerate the tart until firm.

Arrange the raspberries on the top and glaze them with the jam if desired.

BERRY GALETTE WITH SPICE CRUST

Rhubarb and raspberries are a perfect team. Adjust the sweetness level according to the raspberries' tartness.

450g/1lb rhubarb, trimmed and cut into 2.5cm/1in slices
350g/12oz raspberries
150-200g/5-7oz granulated sugar (dependent on the tartness of the fruit)
40g/1½oz plain flour
1 tbsp fresh lemon juice
1 tsp grated lemon rind
15g/½oz butter, melted
1 tsp granulated sugar
1 quantity Spicy Galette Pastry (see page 61), unbaked

Preheat the oven to 200°C/400°F/Gas 6. Line a baking sheet with parchment paper.

Toss the rhubarb, raspberries, sugar, flour and lemon juice and rind together. Set aside.

Roll out the pastry into a 36cm/14in round and flip it on to the prepared baking sheet. Pile the filling into the centre of the pastry, spreading it to about 5cm/2in from the edge. Fold the edge over the filling, pleating the pastry and pressing it to seal. Brush the edge with melted butter and sprinkle with the remaining sugar.

Bake the galette for 45-50 minutes until the filling is bubbling and the crust is browned.

PENNSYLVANIA DUTCH APPLE TORTE

Delicious any time of the year! Choose a firm, tart apple, like Granny Smith, for best flavour and presentation.

275g/10oz plain flour
1 tsp ground cinnamon
¼ tsp ground nutmeg
225g/8oz unsalted butter, at room temperature
200g/7oz granulated sugar
2 eggs, size 3
2 tsp fresh lemon juice
1 tsp vanilla essence
50g/2oz almonds, finely chopped
2 apples, peeled, cored and thinly sliced
25g/1oz flaked almonds

Preheat the oven to 180°C/350°F/Gas 4. Grease and flour a 23cm/9in springclip cake tin.

Sift together the flour, cinnamon and nutmeg. Set aside. In a separate bowl, beat together the butter and sugar until creamy and light in colour. Add the eggs, one at a time, then stir in the lemon juice and vanilla essence. Stir in the dry ingredients and the almonds, being careful not to over-mix. Reserve about 175ml/6fl oz of the mixture and spread the rest into the prepared tin.

Arrange the apple slices decoratively on top of the mixture, leaving a gap of about 1cm/½in to the top of the tin. Pipe or drop the remaining mixture round the edges to make a border. Gently tap the tin on the work surface to release any air bubbles. Sprinkle the almonds on top of the border, pressing them in slightly.

Bake in the centre of the oven for 60-65 minutes until golden brown and a skewer inserted into the centre comes out clean. Allow the torte to cool on a rack for about 15 minutes before releasing it from the tin.

Right: Apricot Upside-Down Gingerbread

ORANGE SUNSHINE CAKE

For an extra orange treat, fill the centre of this golden cake with orange sections and slices of kiwi fruit. It makes a spectacular presentation!

CAKE:

425g/15oz plain flour
3 tsp baking powder
½ tsp salt
225g/8oz unsalted butter, at room temperature

275g/10oz granulated sugar
4 eggs, size 3, separated
225ml/8fl oz fresh orange juice
1 tsp pure orange essence
1 tsp grated orange rind

GLAZE:

250ml/8fl oz fresh orange juice
200g/7oz granulated sugar

Preheat the oven to 180°C/350°F/Gas 4. Grease and flour a 25cm/10in Kugelhopf tin or deep ring mould.

Sift together the flour, baking powder and salt. Set aside. In a separate bowl, beat the butter until creamy. Add the sugar and continue beating until light and fluffy. Beat in the egg yolks, one at a time.

Alternately fold the sifted dry ingredients and the orange juice, orange essence and rind into the butter mixture, beginning and ending with dry ingredients. Be careful not to over-mix or the mixture will curdle.

In another bowl, beat the egg whites until stiff but not dry. Fold these into the orange mixture and pour it into the prepared tin or ring mould. Tap the tin gently on the work surface to remove any air bubbles. Bake in the centre of the oven for 40-45 minutes until a skewer inserted in the centre comes out clean.

Whilst the cake is baking, stir the glaze ingredients together over a low heat until the sugar has dissolved. Set the saucepan aside to cool.

Remove the cake from the oven and allow it to cool in the tin on a wire rack for 10 minutes. Gently poke holes into the cake and spoon about half the glaze over the cake. Allow it to sit for a further 15 minutes. Invert the cake on to a wire rack fitted over a deep plate or a Swiss roll tin and remove the tin. Slowly spoon or brush the remaining glaze over the entire cake surface.

APPLE GALETTE

Any firm, flavoursome apple will do for this rustic-style dessert. Cranberries add colour and tartness (see variation). This recipe is also attractive when the pastry is shaped as individual tartlets.

900g/2lb dessert apples, peeled, cored and cut into 2cm/¾in chunks
50ml/2fl oz apple juice
1 tbsp fresh lemon juice
65g/2½oz granulated sugar
¼ tsp ground cinnamon

1 tsp vanilla essence
65g/2½oz granulated sugar
1½ tbsp cornflour
1 quantity Spicy Galette Pastry (see page 61), unbaked

Preheat the oven to 200°C/400°F/Gas 6. Line a baking sheet with parchment paper.

Combine the apples, apple juice, lemon juice, sugar, cinnamon and vanilla essence in a saucepan and bring to the boil. In a cup, stir the cornflour with a little water to make a paste. Add this to the apple mixture, stir until thickened and boiling. Set aside to cool.

Roll out the pastry into a 30cm/12in round and transfer it to the prepared baking sheet. Pile the filling into the centre of the pastry and fold the edges over themselves, pressing to seal.

Bake in the centre of the oven for 45-50 minutes until the apples are tender and the crust is browned.

CRANBERRY VARIATION:

Add 100g/4oz whole cranberries and an additional 75g/3oz granulated sugar to the apples in the saucepan. Proceed as instructed for the rest of the recipe.

CRANBERRY-PEAR TART

The maple syrup is the key to success with this tart. Don't skimp – use the best!

1¼ tsp powdered gelatine
2 tbsp water
75g/3oz soft brown sugar
175g/6oz whole cranberries
Pinch of ground cinnamon
1 small, ripe pear, peeled, cored and coarsely chopped

3 tbsp pure maple syrup, plus extra for drizzling
½ quantity Classic Pie and Tart Pastry (see page 58), baked blind in a 32cm/9in tart tin with a removable base
350ml/12fl oz Pastry Cream (see page 58)

Dissolve the gelatine with 1 tablespoon of the water. Combine the sugar and remaining water in a saucepan and bring to the boil, stirring to dissolve the sugar. Stir in the cranberries, then the gelatine and cinnamon. Cook, stirring constantly, until the berries begin to pop. Remove the saucepan from the heat and stir in the pear and maple syrup. Chill, stirring occasionally, until the mixture thickens.

Fill the tart case with the pastry cream and top it with the chilled cranberry mixture. Drizzle with more maple syrup, if desired.

Right: Orange Sunshine Cake

'GRAPE-FRUIT' CURD TART

This tart may seem a bit silly and child-like, yet the results are anything but! Use at least two different colours of grapes.

1 quantity Grapefruit Curd (see page 58) chilled

1 quantity Sweet Tart Pastry (see page 61), baked blind in a 23cm/9in tart tin with a removable base

450-600g/1-1¼ lb seedless grapes, halved

75g/3oz apple jelly, melted (optional)

Spread the grapefruit curd over the base of the pastry case. Decoratively arrange the grape halves on top of the curd. Brush with the apple jelly for a shiny finish, if desired. Cover and chill until required.

DEEP-DISH APPLE CRISP

Old-fashioned goodness at its best! Don't forget the vanilla ice cream!

TOPPING:

120g/4½oz plain flour
50g/2oz rolled oats
150g/5oz soft brown sugar
½ tsp ground cinnamon

100g/4oz unsalted butter, chilled and cut into pieces
50g/2oz chopped nuts (walnuts, pecans or almonds)

FILLING:

1.25kg/2½lb apples (Golden Delicious), peeled, cored and cut into 2.5cm/1in chunks
65g/2½oz granulated sugar

1½ tsp ground cinnamon
¼ tsp ground nutmeg
1 tbsp fresh lemon juice
15g/½oz plain flour

Preheat the oven to 180°C/350°F/Gas 4.

For the topping, combine the flour, oats, sugar and cinnamon in a medium-sized bowl. Add the butter and rub it in with your fingers or a pastry blender until coarse crumbs form. Stir in the nuts and set aside.

For the filling, toss the apple chunks with the remaining ingredients and pile them into a 2 litre/3¼ pint ovenproof dish with sides at least 5cm/2in high. Spread the topping over the surface of the apples.

Bake in the centre of the oven for 60 minutes until the apples are tender. Serve warm.

RASPBERRY CHEESECAKE

Any black or red berries are ideal for this recipe, except blueberries and strawberries. This cheesecake is easy to make and will really impress the crowd! Plan on making it a day or two ahead to give the flavours a chance to mellow.

1.25kg/2½lb high-fat soft cheese, at room temperature
400g/14oz granulated sugar
2 tsp vanilla essence

5 eggs, size 3
150g/5 oz raspberries
25g/1oz plain flour

Preheat the oven to 160°C/325°F/Gas 3. Lightly grease a 23cm/9in round cake tin with straight sides, 7.5cm/3in deep.

Beat the soft cheese until very smooth, scraping down the sides of the bowl frequently. Add the sugar and vanilla essence and beat until thoroughly blended. Stir in the eggs, one at a time. Don't over-mix!

Toss the raspberries with the flour to coat them evenly. Gently fold these into the cheese mixture, then pour it into the prepared tin.

Bake the cheesecake in a water bath placed in the centre of the oven for about 75 minutes, or until the top is firm and jiggles only slightly.

Allow the cheesecake to cool in the tin completely before inverting it on to a flat plate. Place a serving plate on the bottom of the cake and invert it again. Refrigerate for at least 8 hours before serving.

APPLE SPICE CAKE

This dark and spicy teacake keeps for a week if tightly wrapped. Children love to find a piece in their lunch box!

175g/6oz unsalted butter, at room temperature
275g/10oz soft brown sugar
2 eggs, size 3
500g/1lb 2oz Apple Sauce (see page 52)
1 tsp vanilla essence
425g/15oz plain flour

1 tbsp baking soda
1 tbsp ground cinnamon
½ tsp ground nutmeg
½ tsp salt
65g/2½oz raisins
2 tbsp Calvados or brandy
50g/2oz chopped pecans, toasted

Preheat the oven to 180°C/350°F/Gas 4. Grease and flour a 25cm/10in Kugelhopf tin or deep ring mould.

Beat the butter and sugar together until light and fluffy. Beat in the eggs, one at a time. Stir in apple sauce and vanilla essence. In a separate bowl, sift together all the dry ingredients before stirring them into the mixture. Add the raisins, Calvados and pecans, stirring until just combined. Pour this into the prepared tin. Bake for 45-40 minutes until a skewer inserted in the centre comes out clean.

Leave the cake in the tin on a rack to cool to room temperature before inverting on to a serving plate.

Right: 'Grape-Fruit' Curd Tart

CHOCOLATE ROLL CAKE WITH STRAWBERRY FOOL

No simpler dessert exists! Garnish the top with picture-perfect strawberries and a few chocolate curls.

6 eggs, size 3, separated
150g/5oz caster sugar
50g/2oz cocoa powder

½ quantity Strawberry Fool (see page 38)
Icing sugar and large block of plain chocolate for garnish

Preheat the oven to 180°C/350°F/Gas 4. Lightly grease a 29 x 18cm/11½ x 7in Swiss roll tin, about 2.5cm/1in deep. Line the base with baking parchment.

Place the egg yolks in a bowl and whisk with an electric hand-held whisk until they begin to thicken. Add the caster sugar and continue to whisk – but be careful not to over-whisk! Fold in the cocoa powder.

In a separate bowl, whisk the egg whites until soft peaks form. Take 1 tablespoon of egg white and gently fold it into the cocoa mixture to slacken it. Then carefully fold in the rest of the egg white. Pour the mixture into the prepared tin and bake it in the middle of the oven for 20-25 minutes until it is springy in the centre. Allow the cake to cool completely on a wire rack in the tin.

Meanwhile, sprinkle a clean tea towel with icing sugar. Immediately invert the cake on to the towel and peel off the paper. Fill the cake with strawberry fool and gently roll up the cake with the help of the tea towel, then place it on a serving plate. Refrigerate at least 6 hours before serving. To garnish, chill the block of chocolate and use a vegetable peeler to shave off curls. Dust the top of the cake with icing sugar, then pile on the curls just before serving.

PEAR TART

Make sure you also try this custard-based tart with your favourite apple. It's easy to make and quick to disappear.

½ quantity Classic Pie and Tart Pastry
(see pages 61), baked blind in a 23cm/9in
tart tin with a removable base
2 ripe medium pears, peeled, cored and
thinly sliced

150ml/5fl oz double cream
50g/2oz + 1 tbsp granulated suga
2 eggs, size 3
1 tsp vanilla essence
1 tbsp dark rum

Preheat the oven to 180°C/350°F/Gas 5.

Leave the tart case in the tart tin and arrange the pear slices decoratively over the base. Whisk together the remaining ingredients, excluding the 1 tablespoon of sugar, to make the custard. Pour it over the pears.

Bake the tart in the centre of the oven for 35-40 minutes until the custard is set. If desired, sprinkle the remaining sugar over the tart and place it under a hot grill for a few minutes to glaze.

APPLE PEAR PIE

A classic American favourite. Dress up this dessert with a lattice topping or just have a simple 'lid'. Either way, serve it with vanilla ice cream!

1 quantity Classic Pie and Tart Pastry
(see page 61), unbaked
900g/2lb dessert apples, peeled, cored,
cut into 5mm/¼in slices
450g/1 lb dessert pears, peeled, cored,
cut into 1cm/½in slices

25g/1oz plain flour
2 tsp ground cinnamon
2 tsp fresh lemon juice
1 tsp vanilla essence
1 egg, size 3, beaten with 1 tbsp water

Preheat the oven to 190°C/375°F/Gas 5. Adjust the shelf to the lowest level in the oven. Roll out and line a 23cm/9in pie dish with half of the pastry and set aside. Roll out the remaining pastry to about 3mm/⅛in thick and cut it into lattice strips (see page 61).

Toss all the remaining ingredients together, except the beaten egg, and pile them into the pastry-lined dish. Arrange the lattice strips across the top and crimp the edges. Using a thin pastry brush, brush the lattice strips with the beaten egg.

Bake for 50-60 minutes until the apples are tender if you pierce then with a skewer through the lattice and the pastry is golden.

BLOOD ORANGE TART

Blood oranges are one of nature's most glamorous fruits. Their season is short so dramatize them when available. The glacé slices in this recipe are also wonderful served alone or as a striking decoration for other desserts. Don't forget, however, to allow enough time to make them the day before you plan to serve this.

200g/7oz granulated sugar
150ml/5fl oz water
2 tbsp light corn syrup
½ vanilla pod, split
3-4 medium blood oranges, sliced
3mm/⅛in thick

1 quantity Sweet Tart Pastry (see
page 61), baked blind in a 23cm/9in
fluted tart tin with a removable base
350ml/12fl oz Pastry Cream (see
page 58)

Combine the sugar, water, corn syrup and vanilla pod in a large frying pan. Bring to the boil, stirring to dissolve the sugar. Reduce the heat and add the orange slices. Simmer for about 10 minutes, swirling the pan occasionally. Remove the pan from the heat and allow it to sit until the orange slices and syrup are cool. Place a rack over a dish and lay the orange slices on it. Refrigerate overnight.

Meanwhile, reduce the syrup until very thick and refrigerate as well.

The next day, fill the tart case with the pastry cream and arrange the orange slices, slightly overlapping, to cover the cream. Gently re-heat the syrup and then brush this over the tart as a glaze.

Right: Chocolate Roll Cake with Strawberry Fool

VIRGINIA SPONGE CAKE WITH FRESH CHERRIES

This is one of the most versatile cakes around! It can be frosted with whipped cream and served with berries, or sliced for summer puddings. Here it is flavoured with lemon and served with Cherry Compôte.

FOR THE CAKE:
6 eggs, size 3, separated
45ml/3 tbsp lemon juice or 2 tsp vanilla extract
2 tsp grated lemon zest (optional)
250g/9oz granulated sugar
¼ tsp cream of tartar
200g/7oz self-raising flour, sifted twice
¼ tsp salt

FOR THE CHERRY COMPÔTE:
450g/1lb red cherries, stoned
450g/1lb white cherries, stoned
150g/6oz granulated sugar
30ml/2 tbsp brandy

Pre-heat the oven to 180°C/350°F/Gas 4. Line the bottom of a 25cm/10in Kubelhopf tin or deep ring mould (2.5 litre/4 ½ pint capacity) with baking parchment.

Beat the egg yolks, lemon juice, grated zest and 200g/7oz of the sugar until thick and fluffy.

Beat the egg whites with the cream of tartar and salt until soft peaks form. Continue beating while gradually adding the sugar. Beat until the whites are stiff and glossy.

Fold one-third of the whites into the yolks to lighten the mixture. Alternately fold in the remaining whites and the flour.

Pour the mixture into the prepared tin. Bake in the centre of the oven for about 50 minutes until golden brown and the cake springs to the touch. Cool completely before removing from the tin.

For the compôte, combine all ingredients. Set aside for at least 2 hours, stirring occasionally.

To serve, cut slices with a serrated knife and garnish with the cherries.

PLUM GALETTE

Dark, plump and juicy plums are perfect for this rustic dessert.

1 quantity Galette Pastry (see page 61)
1.25kg/2½lb ripe plums, stoned and halved
100g/4oz granulated sugar
¼ tsp ground nutmeg
25g/1oz plain flour
1 tsp vanilla essence
1 tbsp lemon juice
Sugar cubes, for garnish

Preheat the oven to 200°C/400°F/Gas 6. Line a baking sheet with parchment paper.

Roll out the galette pastry into a 30cm/12in round. Transfer the pastry to the baking sheet.

In a large bowl, combine all the other ingredients. Pile this filling into the centre of the dough, leaving a 5cm/2in rim of dough uncovered. Fold the rim on itself, as if pleating. Press to seal the edges. Coarsely crush the sugar cubes and press around the edges of the dough.

Bake in the centre of the oven for about 50 minutes until the fruit is tender and the crust browned.

KEY LIME CHIFFON PIE

Key limes are plentiful in the southern American states, and the juice is sold bottled. If you can't find Key limes or their juice, use ordinary limes instead. Be sure to prepare the pretzel crust before you begin the filling so it has plenty of time to chill and set.

1 tbsp powdered gelatine
50ml/2fl oz water
1 quantity Lemon Curd (see page 58) made with Key lime juice instead of lemon juice
5 egg whites, size 3
40g/1½oz granulated sugar
120ml/4fl oz double cream, whipped
1 quantity Pretzel Crust (see page 60), prepared in a 23cm/9in pie plate

TO DECORATE:
Whipped cream and pretzels

Dissolve the gelatine in the water. Either prepare the Key lime curd now and leave it in the saucepan, or return the prepared curd to a saucepan and heat it gently. Stir in the gelatine until it is dissolved. Remove the pan from the heat and transfer the curd mixture to a bowl to cool to room temperature, stirring frequently.

When the curd has cooled and thickened, place the egg whites into a separate bowl and whisk until soft peaks form. Gradually add the sugar and continue whisking until glossy. Fold the curd into the whites along with the whipped cream.

Pour the mixture into the pastry case. Chill for at least 4 hours before serving. Garnish the pie with whipped cream and pretzels.

Right: Plum Galette

BLACKBERRY-RHUBARB PIE

Every time my friend Ann Mileti makes this pie, the neighbourhood is quickly on her doorstep. There is no mistaking the aroma of this freshly baked treat. I always lay a couple of pieces of foil underneath the pie to catch any drippings.

½ quantity Classic Pie and Tart Pastry (see page 61), unbaked
600g/1¼lb rhubarb, trimmed and cut into 2.5cm/1in chunks
275g/10oz granulated sugar
1 tbsp cornflour
3 tbsp water
450g/1 lb blackberries, rinsed and dried
1 egg yolk, size 3
1 tbsp double cream

Preheat the oven to 190°C/375°F/Gas 5. Adjust the shelf to the lowest level in oven. Roll out and line a 23cm/9in pie dish with half of the pastry. Set aside. Roll out the remaining pastry about 3mm/⅛in thick and cut out lattice strips (see page 61).

In a large saucepan, combine the rhubarb and sugar and simmer over a medium-low heat for 7-10 minutes until the rhubarb is just tender but not falling apart.

In a small bowl, stir the cornflour and water together to make a smooth paste. Stir the paste into the rhubarb mixture and cook, stirring constantly, until thickened and boiling. Remove the pan from the heat and gently stir in the blackberries.

Spoon the filling into the pastry case. Arrange the lattice strips across the top and crimp the edges. Beat together the egg yolk and cream and brush over the lattice.

Bake for about 50 minutes until the top is golden brown.

MILE-HIGH LEMON MERINGUE PIE

The tart and tangy curd filling is the perfect foil for the billows of meringue topping. The secret to a 'no weep' meringue is two-fold: one, always top with meringue while the curd is still hot and two, always make sure the meringue touches the edges of the crust. This way the meringue cooks on the bottom from the hot curd and sticks to the edges to prevent shrinking.

2 quantities Lemon Curd (see page 58)
½ quantity Classic Pie and Tart Pastry (see page 61), baked blind in a 23cm/9in tart tin with removable base
5 egg whites, size 3
40g/1½oz granulated sugar

Preheat the oven to 190°C/375°F/Gas 5. Pour the hot lemon curd into the pastry case and set aside.

Whisk the egg whites until soft peaks form. Gradually add the sugar and continue whisking until stiff and glossy. Pile the meringue on to the warm curd, making sure it reaches the edge of the pastry. Swirl the top decoratively.

Bake in the middle of the oven for 20-25 minutes until the meringue is brown and puffed.

MRS BELL'S RHUBARB CUSTARD PIE

In this recipe the rhubarb caramelizes while the pie bakes, providing a nice contrast to the custard. If time is short, skip the lattice work and top it with decorative pastry cut-outs instead.

1 quantity Classic Pie and Tart Pastry (see page 61), unbaked
450g/1lb rhubarb, coarsely chopped
275g/10oz granulated sugar
2 eggs, size 3
3 tbsp plain flour
15g/½oz unsalted butter, melted
¼ tsp ground nutmeg

FOR THE EGG WASH:
1 egg, size 1
1 tbsp single cream

Preheat the oven to 230°C/450°F/Gas 8. Adjust the shelf to the lowest level in the oven.

Roll out and line a 23cm/9in pie dish with half the pastry and set aside. Roll out the remaining pastry to about 3mm/1/8in thick and cut into lattice strips.

Pile the rhubarb into the pie dish. Whisk together the sugar, eggs, flour, butter and nutmeg until smooth. Pour this custard mixture over rhubarb. Arrange the lattice strips across the top and crimp the edges. In a small bowl, mix together the remaining egg and the cream and use this to brush over the pastry.

Bake the pie for 10 minutes. Reduce the temperature to 180°C/350°F/Gas 4 and bake for a further 30 minutes, or until a knife inserted near the centre comes out clean.

PLUM-ALMOND TART

A ripe plum or apricot is the jewel in any frangipane tart. Make sure you try both versions of this recipe!

75g/3oz granulated sugar
75g/3oz flaked almonds, toasted
50g/2oz unsalted butter, at room temperature
1 egg, size 3
1 tsp vanilla essence
1 quantity Sweet Tart Pastry (see page 60), baked blind in a 23cm/9in tart tin
3-4 ripe, firm plums, cut into 1cm/½in slices

Preheat the oven to 190°C/375°F/Gas 5.

In a food processor, combine the sugar and almonds and process until well ground. Add the butter and process until smooth. Add the egg and vanilla extract and process until just combined. Spread this almond filling into the pastry case. Arrange the fruit decoratively on top.

Bake in the centre of the oven for 40-45 minutes until the fruit is tender and the filling is light brown.

APRICOT VARIATION:
Substitute apricot slices for the plums and add a pinch of cinnamon to the almond filling. Proceed as directed above.

Right: Blackberry-Rhubarb Pie

LEMON CURD TART

Any spring or summer fruit will be beautiful atop this delicious tart.

1 quantity Lemon Curd (see page 58)
½ quantity Classic Pie or Tart Pastry
(see page 61), baked blind in a 23cm/9in
tart tin with a removable base

450g/1lb strawberries, hulled if large,
rinsed and dried
Icing sugar and lemon rind, to decorate

Spread the lemon curd into the pastry case. Cut thin strips of lemon rind and arrange in criss-crosses on top. Arrange the strawberries decoratively on the top. Sprinkle with icing sugar.

FRUIT TORTE

Super fast and super easy, this versatile little cake accommodates many different fruits and occasions.

100g/4oz unsalted butter, at room
temperature
150g/5oz + 1 tbsp granulated sugar
2 eggs, size 3
½ tsp vanilla essence
215g/7½oz plain flour

1 tsp baking powder
¼ tsp salt
120ml/4fl oz milk
100g/4oz raspberries, blueberries or
blackberries, or 2 plums or 1 peach,
thinly sliced

Preheat the oven to 180°C/350°F/Gas 4. Lightly grease and flour a 20cm/8in square cake tin, 5cm/2in deep.

Beat the butter and 150g/5oz of the sugar until light and fluffy. Add the eggs and the vanilla essence.

In a separate bowl, combine the dry ingredients. Alternately add the milk and dry ingredients to the butter mixture until just blended. Spoon the mixture into the prepared cake tin.

Arrange the berries or sliced fruit on the top and sprinkle with the remaining sugar. Bake in the centre of the oven for about 45 minutes until golden and a skewer inserted in centre comes out clean.

FRUITY UPSIDE-DOWN CAKE

Vary the fruited topping according to season. This should serve 4- 6.

FOR THE CARAMEL:
90g/3 ½oz granulated sugar
50ml/2fl oz water

FOR THE CAKE:
1 quantity Fruit Torte Cake mixture
(see left), omitting the fruit and only
using 100g/4oz sugar

2-3 plums, sliced, or 400g/14oz cherries,
stoned and halved

Preheat the oven to 180°C/350°F/Gas 4. Lightly grease a 20cm/8in square cake tin, 5cm/2in deep.

Prepare the caramel according to directions in Coconut Crème Caramel (see page 41). Pour the caramel into the prepared baking tin and allow it to stand for 5 minutes to set. Arrange the fruit decoratively on top of the caramel and set aside.

Prepare the fruit torte cake mixture according to the instructions, using only 100g/4oz of sugar. Spoon the mixture evenly over the fruit in the cake tin.

Bake the cake in the centre of the oven for about 45 minutes, or until golden and a skewer inserted in the centre comes out clean. Immediately invert the pan on to a serving dish, allowing the caramel to drip down the sides.

APRICOT CHEESECAKE

Sulphured apricots retain their bright orange colour and give this cheesecake a distinctive look. This recipe should serve about 8.

120g/4½oz digestive biscuits,
finely crushed
120g/4½ oz unsalted butter, melted
1 tbsp grated orange rind
175g/6oz dried apricots
1 tbsp Cointreau or similar

750g/1½lb cream cheese, at room
temperature
150g/5oz granulated sugar
4 eggs, size 3
120ml/4fl oz soured cream
1 tsp vanilla essence

Preheat the oven to 160°C/325°F/Gas 3. Lightly grease a 23cm/9in springclip baking tin.

Combine the crumbs, butter and orange rind and press into the base and about 2.5cm/1in up the side of the pan.

Cover the apricots with water and simmer for about 20 minutes until very tender. Drain them well and finely chop them before tossing with the Cointreau. Set aside.

Beat the cream cheese until very smooth. Add sugar and continue beating until fluffy. Add the eggs, one at a time. Stir in the apricots, soured cream and vanilla. Spoon the mixture into the baking tin.

Bake in a water bath for about 1 hour until the top is firm to the touch and the cake jiggles slightly. Leave it to cool to room temperature before removing from the tin.

Right: Lemon Curd Tart

PUDDINGS, CUSTARDS, TEATIME TREATS

Many of these recipes can be served as a dessert to follow a meal or as an afternoon pick-me-up served with a cup of tea and, thanks to the fruit, they are soothing and satisfying with just the right touch of richness.

RICE PUDDING WITH DRIED CHERRIES

Creamy, rich rice pudding made the old-fashioned way. When serving the pudding chilled, stir in some milk or cream to lighten.

475ml/16fl oz milk
475ml/16fl oz single cream
4 strips of orange rincd
75g/3oz pudding rice
75g/3oz granulated sugar

Pinch of salt
100g/4oz dried cherries
1 tsp vanilla essence
50-120ml/2-4fl oz milk or double cream (optional)

Combine the milk, single cream and orange rind in a saucepan. Bring it to the boil, then slowly stir in the rice. Reduce the heat and simmer for about 35 minutes, stirring frequently, until the rice is very tender. Add the sugar, salt and cherries. Cook for a further 15 minutes until the cherries are tender. Stir in the vanilla.

Serve warm or chilled, adding the milk or double cream if the pudding is chilled.

BLUEBERRY CORNBREAD

Serve these wedges at an afternoon brunch or a southwestern-style dinner party.

120g/4½oz coarse yellow cornmeal
150g/5oz plain flour
100g/4oz granulated sugar
2½ tsp baking powder
¼ tsp salt

175ml/6fl oz buttermilk
1 egg, size 3
150g/5oz unsalted butter, melted and cooled
100g/4oz blueberries, lightly mashed

Preheat the oven to 190°C/375°F/Gas 5. Grease a 23cm/9in pie dish. Combine the cornmeal, flour, sugar, baking powder and salt in a medium-sized bowl. In another bowl, mix together the remaining ingredients. Pour the wet ingredients into the dry and toss them gently to combine. Spread the mixture into the pie dish.

Bake in the centre of the oven for about 35 minutes until golden brown and the centre springs back when touched.

STRAWBERRY SHORTCAKE WITH RHUBARB FOOL

The essential summer dessert! Substitute Strawberry Fool (see page 38) for the rhubarb for an extra-strawberry treat. Serves 6.

350g/12oz strawberries, sliced
25g/1oz granulated sugar
1 tbsp fresh lemon juice

1 quantity Shortcakes pastry (see page 61), baked in a 23cm/9in round (it should take about 25 minutes), cooled
1 quantity Rhubarb Fool (see page 41)

Toss the strawberries with the sugar and the lemon juice. Chill for at least 1 hour, stirring occasionally.

Just before serving, gently slice the shortcake in half horizontally. Place the bottom half on a serving plate and spread about two-thirds of the rhubarb fool over the layer. Spoon half the fruit and juices on top of the fool. Top with the remaining shorcake layer. Dollop the fool on top and garnish with the remaining strawberries and juices.

BLUEBERRY PUDDING

Sprinkle the bread slices with 2 or 3 tablespoons of sherry just before adding the hot berries to make the alcohol flavour more prominent.

10 slices thin stale white bread, no crusts　　*3 tbsp fresh lemon juice*
700g/24oz blueberries　　*1 tbsp grated lemon rind*
200-275g/7-10oz granulated sugar　　*3 tbsp very dry sherry (optional)*

Line a 1 litre/1¾ pint bowl with the bread slices (reserving some slices for the topping), slightly overlapping to ensure there are no holes.

Combine the blueberries, sugar and lemon juice and rind in a saucepan and simmer until the sugar has dissolved and the berries are tender and juicy. Sprinkle the bread with the sherry, if using. Spoon the hot berries into the bread-lined bowl and top with the remaining bread.

Cover the pudding with clingfilm and top with a plate or cardboard. Place a 450g/1lb weight on top and refrigerate the pudding for at least 10 hours.

CITRUS CRISP COOKIES

This refreshing, light snap cookie can also be made into small cups to hold sorbets or firm mousses. To do this, spread the batter to the desired size and bake. Remove them from the baking sheet immediately and mould each cookie on upside-down coffee cups.

215g/7½oz plain flour　　*250g/9oz granulated sugar*
½ tsp salt　　*2 eggs, size 3*
1½ tsp grated citrus rind, such as lime,　　*1¼ tsp lemon essence*
orange or lemon – any combination is nice)
175g/6oz unsalted butter, at room
temperature

Preheat the oven to 180°C/350°F/Gas 4. Line 2 baking sheets with parchment paper.

Sift together the flour and salt, then stir in the rind. Beat the butter and sugar together until light and fluffy. Add the eggs, one at a time. Stir in the lemon juice before folding in the dry ingredients.

Pipe or drop tablespoonfuls of the mixture 5cm/2in apart on to the baking sheets.

Bake for 8-10 minutes until golden around the edges. Remove the cookies from the baking sheets and place on a rack to cool completely.

CLASSIC CHERRY CLAFOUTI

Nothing beats the classic version of this pudding dessert – except, maybe, the peach variation below.

65g/2½oz + 2 tablespoons granulated　　*50ml/2fl oz soured cream*
sugar　　*3 eggs, size 3*
350g/12oz cherries, stems and stones　　*225ml/8fl oz milk*
removed　　*1 tsp vanilla essence*
65g/2½oz plain flour　　*15g/½oz unsalted butter, at room*
Pinch of salt　　*temperature*

Preheat the oven to 190°C/375°F/Gas 5. Grease a 23cm/9in shallow ovenproof dish and sprinkle it with 1 tablespoon of the sugar. Arrange the cherries over the base.

Sift together the flour, 65g/2½oz sugar and salt. Stir together the soured cream, eggs, milk and vanilla. Whisk these ingredients into the dry ingredients until smooth.

Pour this mixture over the fruit. Dot the pudding with the butter and the remaining 1 tablespoon of sugar. Bake for 40-45 minutes until puffed and brown. Serve warm.

PEACH ALMOND VARIATION:
Cut 450g/1lb ripe peaches into 1cm/½in slices and toss with 25g/1oz granulated sugar and 15g/½oz plain flour. Arrange the fruit on the base of a dish prepared as above. Stir in ¼ tsp almond essence. Pour the mixture over the fruit and top the pudding with 50g/2oz sliced almonds. Bake as above.

SHORTCAKES WITH CARAMELIZED PEARS AND GINGER CREAM

Who says shortcake is just for the summer time? Caramelized pears and ginger cream lend a warm earthy feel to the traditional shortcake. This recipe makes 8.

1 quantity Shortcakes (see page 60)
baked and cooled

FOR THE PEARS:
50g/2oz unsalted butter
4 firm, ripe pears, peel, cored and cut
into 1cm/½in slices

65g/2½oz granulated sugar
¼ tsp fresh lemon juice

FOR THE GINGER CREAM:
350ml/12fl oz double cream
50g/2oz granulated sugar

2 tsp vanilla essence
½ tsp ground ginger

To caramelize the pears, melt the butter in a large frying pan over a medium-low heat. Arrange the pears in the pan so they barely overlap and sprinkle them with the sugar and lemon juice. Sauté the slices, turning them regularly, for 20-25 minutes until caramelized. Keep them at room temperature.

Whip the cream, gradually adding the sugar, until semi-firm peaks form. Stir in the vanilla essence and the ginger.

To serve, separate the shortcakes in half and layer them with the pears and cream.

CRANBERRY SCONES

A cheery alternative to the original scone. Currants can easily be substituted for the cranberries. This recipe makes 6.

40g/1½oz dried cranberries
65ml/2½fl oz fresh orange juice
275g/10oz plain flour
2 tsp baking powder
¼ tsp salt

50g/2oz granulated sugar
100g/4oz unsalted butter, chilled
and diced
175ml/6fl oz buttermilk

Preheat the oven to 200°C/400°F/Gas 6. Line a baking sheet with parchment paper.

Combine the cranberries and orange juice in a saucepan and bring to the simmer. Remove from the heat and let them sit for 15 minutes.

Meanwhile, in a separate bowl, combine the flour, baking powder, salt and 3 tablespoons of the sugar. Rub in the butter to form coarse crumbs. Drain the cranberries, reserving the liquid, and add them with the buttermilk to the crumbs, tossing gently to combine.

Shape the scone dough into a flat 20cm/8in circle. Cut this into 6 triangles. Brush with the reserved juice and sprinkle with the remaining sugar. Bake on the parchment-lined baking sheet for 18 minutes, or until puffed and golden brown. Serve straight from the oven or at room temperature.

Above: *Mango-Raspberry Shortcakes*

MANGO-RASPBERRY SHORTCAKES

To get clean slices of mango, refer to the instructions given in Helpful Hints for Handling Fruit (see page 10). This recipe makes 8 scrumptious shortcakes.

2 ripe mangoes, sliced
325g/11oz raspberries
50g/2oz granulated sugar
1 tsp grated lime rind
1-2 tbsp Cointreau or similar
1 tsp vanilla essence

475ml/16fl oz double cream
1 quantity Shortcakes (see page
61), with ½ tsp ground nutmeg
added to the dry ingredients, baked and
cut into eight 7.5cm/3in rounds

Combine the mangoes and raspberries with the sugar, lime rind and Cointreau. Toss everything together and set aside for at least 1 hour.

Just before serving, add the vanilla to the cream and whip until soft peaks form. Split the shortcakes in half and layer them with the whipped cream and fruit. Serve at once.

PEACH COBBLER

Summer peaches are never more delicious than when tossed with a bit of sugar and topped with a light and puffy buttermilk crust.

FILLING:

1.5kg/3lb ripe peaches, cut into	*1 tbsp fresh lemon juice*
1cm/½in slices	*25g/1oz plain flour*
50-75g/2-3oz granulated sugar	
(amount depends on sweetness of peaches)	

TOPPING:

215g/7½oz plain flour	*1 egg, size 3, beaten*
50-65g/2-2½oz granulated sugar	*150ml/5fl oz buttermilk*
2½ tsp baking powder	*75g/3oz unsalted butter, melted*
¼ tsp salt	*and cooled*

Preheat the oven to 190°C/375°F/Gas 5. Lightly grease a 2-2.5 litre/3¼-4 pint ovenproof dish. In a large bowl, toss all the filling ingredients together, then spoon them into the prepared dish.

To make the topping, combine the flour, sugar, baking powder and salt in a medium-sized bowl. Add the remaining ingredients and toss gently to blend into a dough. Drop heaped spoonfuls of the mixture on to the fruit to cover.

Bake the cobbler in the centre of the oven for about 40 minutes until it is golden brown on top and the filling is bubbly.

BANANA WAFFLES

These waffles freeze beautifully. Layer them with tin foil and freeze them for up to 3 months. Reheat them from frozen under the grill. They're delicious topped with whipped cream and sliced bananas.

275g/10oz plain flour	*125ml/4fl oz soured cream*
40g/2½oz granulated sugar	*300ml/10fl oz milk*
21/2 tsp baking powder	*100g/4oz butter, melted*
¾ tsp bicarbonate of soda	*75ml/3fl oz sunflower oil*
¾ tsp salt	*1 tsp vanilla essence*
4 eggs, size 3, separated	*50g/2oz walnuts, toasted and chopped*
100g/4oz ripe bananas, mashed	*(optional)*

Heat a waffle iron according to the manufacturer's instructions. Sift the flour, sugar, baking powder, bicarbonate of soda and salt together. In a separate bowl, beat the egg yolks and all the remaining ingredients, except the nuts, until well blended. Stir in the dry ingredients until just blended.

Beat the egg whites until stiff but not dry. Fold the whites and nuts, if using, into the mixture.

Cook according to the waffle manufacturer's instructions.

RASPBERRY DROP MUFFINS

Although these aren't really muffins, the texture is soft and cake-like, similar to that of a classic muffin. Regardless of the name, however, try them with your favourite berry! This recipe makes 8.

150g/5oz plain flour	*50g/2oz unsalted butter, chilled and*
65g/2½oz granulated sugar	*diced*
1½ tsp baking powder	*125ml/4fl oz soured cream*
Pinch of salt	*65g/2½oz raspberries*

Preheat the oven to 190°C/375°F/Gas 5. Lightly grease a baking sheet or line it with parchment paper.

Combine the flour, sugar, baking powder and salt in a medium-sized bowl. Rub in the butter until it forms coarse crumbs. Stir in the soured cream and raspberries until just combined. The dough will be sticky! Drop 8 mounds on to the baking sheet.

Bake the muffins in the centre of the oven for 20-25 minutes until puffed, springy and golden brown.

RED BERRY PUDDING

Thick slices of stale sponge cake are delicious with this berry mix. Stale bread also works well.

14 thick slices stale Virginia	*200g/7oz granulated sugar*
Sponge (see page 24)	*50ml/2fl oz Grand Marnier or similar*
850g/1¾ lb red berries: raspberries	*2 tsp grated lemon rind*
strawberries and redcurrants	

Line a 1.8 litre/3 pint bowl or soufflé dish with the cake slices, filling in any holes, but reserving some of the slices to top the pudding.

Quarter the strawberries. Combine all the ingredients and simmer until the sugar is dissolved and the fruit is tender and juicy. Spoon the mixture into the dish and top with the remaining cake slices.

Cover the pudding with clingfilm and top with a plate. Place a 450g/1 lb weight on the top and refrigerate for at least 10 hours.

Right: Peach Cobbler

BLUEBERRY QUEEN OF PUDDINGS

Taste this little known dessert gem and be ready to fall in love! The traditional version calls for jam, but nothing beats the taste of fresh blueberries. This should serve 6-8.

2 slices stale white bread	*2 tsp grated lemon rind*
550ml/18fl oz milk	*25g/1oz plain flour*
200g/7oz granulated sugar	*3 tbsp fresh lemon juice*
4 egg yolks, size 3	*3 egg whites, size 3*
¼ tsp vanilla essence	*40g/1½ oz granulated sugar*
175g/6 oz blueberries	

Preheat the oven to 180°C/350°F/Gas 4. Grease a 20cm/8in square ovenproof serving dish.

Crumble the bread slices and layer these in the dish. Combine the milk, 90g/3½oz of sugar, the egg yolks and the vanilla essence. Pour this mixture over the bread and allow it to stand for 15 minutes for the bread to swell.

Bake the pudding in the centre of the oven for about 30 minutes until custard is almost set.

Meanwhile, combine blueberries, another 90g/3½oz of sugar, the lemon rind and the flour in a small saucepan. Stir in the lemon juice. Bring to the simmer and continue simmering for about 15 minutes, stirring constantly, until the berries are tender and the liquid is thick. When the custard is baked, carefully spread the blueberries over the top.

Whisk the egg whites until soft peaks form. Gradually add the remaining sugar and continue whisking until glossy. Spoon this over the blueberries. and bake for about 25 minutes until the meringue is puffed and browned.

INDIVIDUAL BLUEBERRY SUMMER PUDDINGS

Thinly sliced bread works best with individual puddings. The fruit is the true star of this dessert. This recipe makes 6.

About 20 thin slices of stale white bread	*1½ tsp ground cinnamon*
800g/1¼lb blueberries	*2 tbsp dry sherry (optional)*
250g/9oz granulated sugar	*Whipped cream, to decorate*

Line 6 ramekins with the bread, reserving some for the toppings. Make sure there are no holes.

Over a low heat, simmer together all the other ingredients until the sugar dissolves and the fruit is tender and juicy. Spoon the mixture into the ramekins and top them with the remaining bread. Cover them with clingfilm and weight each one down. Refrigerate for at least 10 hours.

To serve, invert the puddings and decorate them with whipped cream, if desired.

INDIAN PUDDINGS

A favourite in American comfort foods! Experiment with different types of dried fruits, or just go with raisins! This recipe makes 8.

1 litre/1¼ pints milk	*2 eggs, size 3*
90g/3½oz molasses	*50g/2oz coarse yellow cornmeal*
65g/2½oz soft brown sugar	*75g/3oz dried fruit*

Preheat the oven to 160°C/325°F/Gas 3. Lightly butter 8 ramekins.

Combine the milk, molasses, sugar and eggs in a large saucepan. Whisk them over a medium heat for about 3 minutes until slightly thickened. Gradually whisk in the cornmeal. Simmer, stirring constantly, until the mixture is bubbly and thickened.

Spoon the mixture into the prepared ramekins and top with the dried fruit. Bake the puddings in a water bath for about 60 minutes until set.

Serve warm or chilled.

Right: Individual Blueberry Summer Puddings

MOUSSES, SOUFFLÉS, SABAYONS

Here s a selection of light and airy desserts. Most of the fluffiness comes from the addition of beaten egg whites or cream, or both.

Again, the addition of fruit keeps things fresh tasting, offering the perfect ending to a special meal.

REDCURRANT SOUFFLÉ

For variety, substitute raspberries for half of the redcurrants, reducing the quantity of sugar to about 150g/5oz and strain the purée before folding it into the egg whites.

225g/8oz redcurrants
1tbsp Grand Marnier or similar
200-50g/7-9oz granulated sugar

6 egg whites, size 3
Pinch of salt
Icing sugar, to decorate

Preheat the oven to 190°C/375°F/Gas 5. Grease and sugar a 1 litre/1¾ pint soufflé dish.

Combine the redcurrants, reserving a few for the decoration, Grand Marnier and all but 65g/2½oz of the sugar in a saucepan. Simmer, stirring constantly, until the currants are juicy and the sugar has dissolved. Strain and chill thoroughly.

Whisk the egg whites and salt until soft peaks form. Continue whisking them while gradually adding the remaining sugar and whisk until stiff and glossy. Gently fold the cold purée into the egg whites until well blended. Spoon the mixture into the prepared dish.

Bake in the centre of the oven for 30 minutes until puffed and browned. Decorate with icing sugar and fresh currants. Serve immediately.

BERRY GRATINS

Any combination of fresh, sweet summer berries will be delicious and elegant when topped with a rich sabayon. Don't forget, the sabayon must be whipped up at the last minute. This recipe makes 6.

450g/1lb mixed fresh berries
(quarter strawberries if using)
100g/4oz granulated sugar

Pinch of salt
2 tbsp Marsala wine, sherry, brandy or rum
3 egg yolks, size 3

Divide the berries into 6 shallow flameproof serving dishes. Preheat the grill to medium-high.

Combine the remaining ingredients in a bowl. Set the bowl over simmering water and whisk constantly for about 3 minutes, until the mixture is very thick and creamy.

Spoon this sabayon equally over the berries. Set the dishes on a baking sheet and place under the grill for 3-4 minutes until golden brown. Serve immediately.

APRICOT MOUSSES

Fresh, ripe apricots are essential to this delicate, flavoursome mousse. Garnish each serving with apricot slices and a dessert biscuit. .

1 sachet powdered gelatine
60ml/2¼fl oz fresh orange juice
165g/5½oz apricot purée
65g/2½oz granulated sugar

2 tbsp fresh lemon juice
2 egg whites, whisked
150ml/5fl oz double cream, whipped

Mix the gelatine with the orange juice. In a saucepan, combine the apricot purée, sugar and lemon juice. Simmer, stirring, to dissolve the sugar. Add the dissolved gelatine and stir. Cool the mixture to room temperature and thickened but not set.

Fold in the egg whites and cream. Spoon into serving goblets. Chill for at least 6 hours before serving.

CHOCOLATE SABAYON WITH BLOOD ORANGES

This is one fast dessert! While blood oranges are delicious and beautiful, their season is short. Pineapple makes a terrific substitute.

3 blood oranges, sectioned with all the pith removed
4 eggs, size 3

100g/4oz granulated sugar
3 tbsp brandy
100g/4oz dark chocolate, chopped

Arrange the orange sections on the serving plate and set aside. In a medium-sized bowl, combine the eggs, sugar and brandy. Set the bowl over simmering water and whisk for about 5 minutes until thickened. Remove the bowl from the heat and whisk in the chocolate until smooth. Spoon the sabayon over the oranges and serve immediately.

STRAWBERRY FOOL

Feel free to use any combination of red berries for this super simple, super rich dessert. For a stylish presentation, serve in Citrus Crisp Cookie cups (see page 32) and garnish with a few whole berries.

350g/12oz strawberries, hulled and halved
50g/2oz granulated sugar

½ tsp vanilla essence
300ml/10fl oz double cream

Mash the strawberries, reserving a few for decoration, with the sugar until juicy and coarse. Refrigerate until very cold, then add the vanilla.

Whip the cream until stiff, then fold in the strawberry mixture. Transfer to a serving dish and refrigerate for at least 4 hours, until firmer, before serving.

BLACKBERRY-WHITE CHOCOLATE PARFAITS

Any fresh berry will substitute for the blackberry. Serve the parfait in tall champagne flutes for a dramatic effect. This recipe makes 6.

275g/10oz blackberries
25g/1oz granulated sugar
1 tsp lemon juice
1 sachet powdered gelatine
50ml/2fl oz water
4 eggs, size 3, separated

50g/2oz icing sugar, sifted
100g/4oz white chocolate, chopped
75g/3oz unsalted butter, at room temperature
½ tbsp vanilla essence
250ml/8fl oz double cream, whipped

Toss the berries with the granulated sugar and lemon juice and set aside. Dissolve the gelatine in the water.

Beat the egg yolks and icing sugar in a bowl set in a pan of simmering water for about 4 minutes until very thick. Remove from the heat and stir in the white chocolate, butter, vanilla and dissolved gelatine until melted. Cool to room temperature.

In a separate bowl, beat the egg whites until stiff peaks form. Fold the beaten egg whites and whipped cream into the chocolate-mousse mixture. Spoon or pipe it into 6 glasses, layering it with the fruit.

RASPBERRY-LEMON MOUSSE CAKE

Spring is here! No matter what the season this mousse cake is a real crowd pleaser. Serves 6.

½ baked Genoise Sponge (see page 58), one 1cm/½in layer
1 tbsp Grand Marnier or similar(optional)
1 sachet powdered gelatine
1 quantity Lemon Curd (see page 58), made with 50g/2oz extra sugar

3 egg whites, size 3
100g/4oz granulated sugar
150ml/5fl oz double cream, whipped to soft peaks
100g/4oz raspberries

Fit the Genoise layer in a 23cm/9in springclip cake tin. Sprinkle it with an orange-flavoured liqueur, if desired. Set aside.

Soften the gelatine in the water. Prepare the lemon curd according to instructions. Add the gelatine to the curd and stir until dissolved. Cool until the curd is an egg white consistency.

Beat the egg whites until soft peaks form. Continue beating, gradually adding the sugar, until stiff and glossy. Fold the egg whites and the whipped cream into the cooled lemon curd until blended. Gently fold in the raspberries. Pour the mixture into the cake tin and refrigerate for about 6 hours until firm.

LEMON MOUSSE QUENELLES VARIATION:
Prepare the lemon mousse without the raspberries and chill for at last 4 hours until set. To serve, dip 2 large spoons or an ice-cream scoop into warm water, then scoop up the mousse and mould into egg shapes. Serve with Red Berry Sauce (see page 61).

ORANGE SOUFFLÉ

Molly Stevens, the noted American food writer and instructor, adds a layer of fruit in the middle of the soufflé. It won't rise quite as much but it is well worth it. The pastry cream base of this soufflé can be made in advance; just bring it to room temperature before folding in the whites.

40g/1½oz plain flour
100g/4oz granulated sugar
6 egg yolks, size 3
1 tbsp grated orange rind
3 tbsp Grand Marnier or similar

225ml/8fl oz milk
8 egg whites, size 3
Pinch of salt
1 navel orange, sectioned and with pith removed

Preheat the oven to 190°C/375°F/Gas 5. Grease and sugar a 2 litre/3¼ pint soufflé dish.

Combine the flour, half the sugar, the egg yolks, orange rind and Grand Marnier until well blended. In a saucepan, bring the milk to the simmer before removing the pan from the heat and gradually adding the yolk mixture, stirring constantly. Return the mixture to the heat and simmer, stirring constantly, until thick and bubbling. Transfer the mixture to a bowl and allow to cool to room temperature.

In a separate bowl, beat the egg whites with a pinch of salt until soft peaks form. Gradually add the remaining sugar and continue beating until stiff and glossy. Gently fold in the cooled pastry cream.

Spoon about one-third of the mixture into the prepared dish. Arrange orange sections on top and then spoon over the remaining pastry cream.

Bake in the centre of the oven for about 35 minutes until puffed and browned. Serve immediately.

MANGO FOOL

Is this a fool because any fool can make it, or because you would be a fool not to try this recipe?

2 large ripe mangoes, peeled and cut into chunks
65ml/2½fl oz fresh orange juice
2 tbsp fresh lime juice

Pinch of salt
100-150g/4-5oz granulated sugar
225ml/8fl oz double cream, whipped

TO DECORATE:
Sprig of mint
Toasted hazelnuts

Combine the mango chunks, orange and lime juices, salt and 100g/4oz sugar in a food processor. Pulse until puréed. Taste and add more sugar if desired. Chill for about 2 hours until very cold.

Fold the mango purée into the cream and chill for at least 4 hours before serving. Garnish with a mint sprig and some toasted hazelnuts.

Right: Blackberry-White Chocolate Parfait

ICE CREAMS, SORBETS, GRANITAS

You do not need a special ice-cream maker to prepare these frozen desserts. If you do plan on purchasing a machine, the main choices are those that freeze in the machine and those that require you to transfer the mixture to your freezer compartment. If your freezer compartment is small, then the first option may be the better choice.

BLACKCURRANT GRANITA

A granita is a combination of puréed fruit and a sugar syrup. It differs from its cousin the sorbet simply in texture – a granita is more icy because it tends to have less sugar and is served still frozen. A well-made granita is one of the easiest low-fat desserts in the world! This should serve 4 to 6.

300ml/10fl oz water   *450g/1lb blackcurrants*
200g/7oz granulated sugar

Combine all the ingredients in a saucepan. Simmer gently, stirring constantly until the sugar has dissolved and the currants are soft. Strain through a nylon sieve, if desired.

Pour the mixture into a shallow container and place it in the freezer. Stir the granita every 30 minutes or so until the mixture begins to set.

LEMON SUCKER SORBET

Smooth and delicious, this sorbet truly lives up to its name. Of course, you can taste the syrup before freezing and adjust the sweetness.

350g/12oz granulated sugar   *300ml/10fl oz water*
1 tbsp vodka or 1 egg white, size 4,   *350ml/12fl oz fresh lemon juice*
beaten lightly

Combine the sugar, water and lemon juice in a saucepan. Simmer, stirring, until the sugar is dissolved. Remove the saucepan from the heat and allow it to cool completely.

Stir in the vodka or egg white as preferred. Freeze the sorbet in an ice-cream maker according to the manufacturer's instructions, or place it in a freezerproof bowl in the freezer, stirring frequently to disperse any ice crystals.

WATERMELON ICE

Better than watermelon – no seeds! Check the fruit for sweetness and adjust the sugar as needed.

100g/4oz granulated sugar   *475ml/16fl oz watermelon purée*
120ml/4fl oz water
3 sprigs of mint, or 1 sprig of rosemary
(optional)

Combine the sugar, water and herb, if using, in a medium-sized saucepan. Bring to the boil, stirring to dissolve the sugar. Remove from the heat and allow to cool completely.

Remove the herb and stir in the watermelon purée. Pour the mixture into a shallow freezerproof container and place in the freezer. Stir every 30 minutes or so until the mixture begins to set.

PEACH ICE CREAM

Peaches and cream! Nothing could be more wonderful – unless it's frozen!

4 ripe peaches, peeled, sliced and mashed   *150g/5oz granulated sugar*
350ml/12fl oz double cream   *1 tsp vanilla essence*

Combine the mashed peaches and their juices with the cream and sugar in the saucepan. Simmer, stirring to dissolve the sugar. Remove from the heat and chill thoroughly.before stirring in the vanilla.

Freeze in an ice-cream maker according to the manufacturer's instructions, or place in a freezerproof container in the freezer, stirring frequently to disperse any ice crystals.

PEACH MELBA VARIATION:
100g/4oz raspberries   *2 tsp Triple Sec*
1 tsp granulated sugar

Combine the ingredients, leaving them to soak for 30 minutes. Strain off the juices, if desired, and add, along with the fruit, to the partially frozen ice cream. Return the ice cream to the freezer.

CRANBERRY SORBET

This sweet-tart dessert will quickly become a family favourite at Christmas. But keep a bag or two of cranberries in the freezer so you can enjoy this sorbet all year long!

150g/5oz granulated sugar	*1 tbsp fresh lemon juice*
120ml/4fl oz water	*Pinch of ground cinnamon*
250g/9oz whole cranberries	*1 tbsp vodka or 1 egg white, size 4,*
350ml/12fl oz cranberry juice	*beaten lightly*

Combine the sugar, water and cranberries in a saucepan. Boil for 3 minutes, stirring to dissolve the sugar. Remove the saucepan from the heat and set aside to cool completely.

Process the cranberry mixture in a food processor, then strain it through a fine mesh nylon sieve. Stir in the remaining ingredients.

Freeze the sorbet in an ice-cream maker according to the manufacturer's instructions, or place in a freezerproof container in the freezer, stirring frequently to break up any ice crystals.

FRUITY ICE CREAM

Choose any one of the three fruit combinations to add to this rich and delicious vanilla ice cream. You can add the fruit, juices and all, or strain off the juice and just add the macerated fruit.

VANILLA ICE CREAM:

600ml/1 pint single cream	*150g/5oz granulated sugar*
6 egg yolks, size 3	*1 tsp vanilla essence*

NECTARINE-CINNAMON ICE CREAM:

1 medium-sized nectarine, finely chopped	*1 tsp granulated sugar*
¼ tsp ground cinnamon	*½ tsp brandy*

BANANA-RUM ICE CREAM:

1 ripe banana, mashed	*1 tbsp dark rum*
2 tsp soft brown sugar	

STRAWBERRY ICE CREAM:

8 strawberries, mashed	*½ tsp grated lemon zest*
15g/½oz granulated sugar	

To make the vanilla ice cream, heat the cream in a saucepan until just boiling. Whisk together the egg yolks and sugar. Gradually whisk in the heated cream and then pour the mixture back into the pan. Cook, stirring constantly, over a medium heat until it has thickened and is 77°C/180°F on a jam thermometer. Strain and chill thoroughly.

Meanwhile, combine all the ingredients for your chosen fruit addition and set aside for at least 1 hour.

When the mixture is chilled, stir in the vanilla. Freeze in an ice-cream maker according to the manufacturer's instructions, or place in a freezerproof container in the freezer, stirring frequently to disperse any ice crystals. Strain off the juice, if desired, and add this, along with the fruit, to the mixture halfway through the freezing process.

MANGO GRANITA

Cayenne pepper gives this granita a special zing. It's not too hot, just enough for a contrasting accent to the mellow mango flavour.

225ml/8fl oz water	*1½ tbsp fresh lime juice*
150g/5oz granulated sugar	*1 tsp grated lime rind*
3 very ripe mangoes, peeled, de-stoned,	*Pinch of cayenne pepper*
puréed and strained	*Pinch of salt*

Combine the water and the sugar in saucepan. Bring to the boil, stirring to dissolve the sugar.

Remove the saucepan from the heat and allow to cool completely. Stir in the remaining ingredients. Taste and add a little more cayenne if desired.

Pour the mixture into a shallow container and place it in the freezer. Stir the granita every 30 minutes or so until the mixture begins to set.

PLUM RASPBERRY SORBET

Choose very ripe plums and raspberries for a deep flavoured sorbet.

175ml/6fl oz water	*40g/1½oz raspberries*
150g/5oz granulated sugar	*1 ½ tbsp fresh lemon juice*
750g/1¾lb plums, pitted and cut	*1 tbsp Triple Sec or 1 egg white, size 4,*
into 2cm/¾in chunks	*beaten lightly*

Combine the water, sugar, plums and raspberries in a saucepan. Cover and simmer, stirring often, until the fruit is very soft – this should take about 15 minutes. Pour the mixture through a fine mesh nylon sieve and allow to cool completely. Stir in the remaining ingredients.

Freeze in an ice-cream maker according to the manufacturer's instructions, or place in a freezerproof container in the freezer, stirring frequently to disperse any ice crystals.

CHOCOLATE-CHERRY ICE CREAM

The macerated cherries in this recipe are delicious all on their own or triple the recipe and serve them with the Virginia Sponge (see page 24) instead of fresh berries. Here they are paired with rich chocolate ice cream. You can add the cherry juices or strain it off – either way it's very cherry!

600ml/1 pint single cream
6 egg yolks, size 3
65g/2½oz granulated sugar
225g/8oz dark chocolate, finely chopped

½ tsp vanilla essence
75g/3oz hazelnuts, toasted and chopped (optional)

FOR THE CHERRIES:
225g/8oz cherries, stoned
50g/2oz granulated sugar
1 tbsp brandy

Heat the cream to just below the boiling point. In a medium-sized bowl, whisk together the egg yolks and sugar.

Gradually whisk in the hot cream and chocolate, then pour the mixture back into the saucepan. Cook, stirring constantly, over a medium heat until the mixture is thick and reaches 77°C/180°F on a jam thermometer. Strain the mixture into a bowl and refrigerate it until completely chilled.

Combine the cherry ingredients and let them sit while the cream is cooling.

When the mixture is chilled, stir in the vanilla. Freeze the cooled ice-cream mixture in an ice-cream maker according to directions or freeze, stirring frequently to disperse any ice crystals.

Strain off the cherry juice, if desired, and add this along with the chopped cherries and hazelnuts, if using, to the chocolate mixture halfway through the freezing process.

PINA COLADA ICE CREAM

Just top with toasted coconut and you are halfway to the Caribbean! Allowing the yogurt to drain gives the finished product a smoother consistency – not essential but preferred.

350g/12oz low-fat yogurt
400ml/14fl oz single cream or milk
150g/5oz granulated sugar

175g/6oz pineapple, well drained and finely chopped
1 tbsp dark rum

Drain the yogurt in a muslin-lined sieve set over a bowl for about 1 hour to drain off some of the liquid.

In a saucepan, combine the milk and sugar. Simmer to dissolve the sugar. Transfer to a bowl and set aside to cool. Stir in the strained yogurt, the pineapple and the rum.

Freeze in ice-cream maker according to the manufacturer's instructions, or place in a freezerproof container in the freezer, stirring frequently to disperse any ice crystals.

PINK GRAPEFRUIT SORBET

Refreshing and light, yet loaded with grapefruit flavour! Perfect for a winter dinner intermezzo or a summertime cooler.

4 large pink or ruby red grapefruit
275g/10oz granulated sugar
1 tbsp vodka

1 tbsp fresh lemon juice
Pinch of salt

Cut 3 large strips of rind from the grapefruit (make sure to remove all the white pith). Squeeze the grapefruit and combine the juice with the sugar and rind in a saucepan. Bring to the boil, then simmer until the sugar dissolves. Remove the pan from the heat and allow it to stand for at least 30 minutes for the juice to infuse and cool completely. Remove the rind and stir in the vodka, lemon juice and salt.

Freeze in an ice-cream maker according to the manufacturer's instructions, or place in a freezerproof container in the freezer, stirring frequently to disperse any ice crystals.

MINT-ORANGE TEA SORBET

Ice tea is a favourite drink any time of the year. This sorbet is delicious even when it isn't frozen!

200g/7oz granulated sugar
600ml/1 pint water
6 tea bags
4 sprigs of mint

350ml/12fl oz fresh orange juice
1 tbsp Triple Sec or other orange-flavoured liqueur
1 tbsp vodka

Combine the sugar and water in a saucepan and bring to the boil, then simmer, stirring, until the sugar has dissolved. Remove the saucepan from the heat, add the tea bags and mint sprigs and allow to cool for at least 30 minutes.

Remove the tea bags and mint sprigs before stirring in the orange juice, liqueur and vodka. Freeze the sorbet in an ice-cream maker according to the manufacturer's instructions or place in a freezerproof container in the freezer, stirring frequently to break up any ice crystals.

LIME ICE CREAM

Honey sweetens and mellows the lime flavour in this creamy treat.

2 tbsp clear honey
150g/5oz granulated sugar
120ml/4fl oz fresh lime juice

2 tsp grated lime rind
475ml/16fl oz single cream

Combine the honey, sugar and lime juice and rind in a saucepan. Simmer, stirring, to dissolve the sugar, then remove the pan from the heat and leave the mixture to cool completely. Stir in the cream.

Freeze, following the instructions for Pina Colada Ice Cream (see left).

Right Chocolate-Cherry Ice Cream

FRESH FRUIT AND COMPÔTES

Here is a selection of light and easy fruit desserts. The recipes are easy to follow and the results are stunning, making them the perfect choice for a sophisticated finish to an elegant meal.

POACHED SECKLE PEARS

Seckels are the smallest of pears. Dainty and delicious, they can also be costly. Feel free to substitute larger Comice or Anjou, cutting them in half. The poaching time will vary depending on the size and ripeness of the pears.

1.2 litres/2 pints non-alcoholic cider
150g/6oz soft brown sugar
2 cinnamon sticks, about 7.5cm/3in long

½ vanilla pod, split
6 firm Seckel pears or 3 Comice, peeled and cored from the bottom

Combine all the ingredients, except for the pears, in a medium-sized saucepan, just big enough to hold the pears when they are required. Simmer, stirring, until the sugar has dissolved.

Add the pears and cover with a piece of baking parchment paper to keep the fruit down. Simmer for 10-25 minutes, turning the pears over occasionally, until they are tender. Cool to room temperature, then cover the saucepan and refrigerate until throughly chilled.

Before serving, remove the pears and boil the poaching liquid until thick and syrupy.

Serve the pears drizzled with some of the liquid.

APRICOT VARIATION:
Stuff each pear cavity with 1 or 2 dried apricots before poaching and continue as directed above.

STEWED STONE FRUIT

Make use of early, firmer fruit for this light dessert. Garnish the fruit with a chiffonade of fresh mint leaves just before serving.

2 ripe-yet-firm peaches
3 ripe-yet-firm plums
4 ripe-yet-firm apricots
2 ripe-yet-firm nectarines

2 tbsp fresh lemon juice
150g/5oz granulated sugar
225ml/8fl oz water
3 sprigs of fresh mint

Cut all the fruit into 2cm/3/4in thick sections – there's no need to peel! Toss with the lemon juice and set aside.

Combine the sugar and water in a large saucepan. Simmer to dissolve the sugar. Add the fruit and simmer for about 10 minutes, stirring occasionally, until all the fruit is just tender. Remove from the heat and add the mint sprigs.

Cool to room temperature, then cover and chill overnight before serving.

WINTER FRUIT COMPÔTE

Spoon this wintry treat over a piece of Orange Sunshine Cake (see page 18) or with a dollop of whipped cream.

475ml/16fl oz dry white wine
½ vanilla pod, split
225g/8oz dried Black Mission figs, cut in half
225g/8oz dried Calamyrna figs, cut in half

250g/9oz dried apricots, cut in half
165g/5½oz raisins
100g/4oz fresh cranberries
150-200g/5-7oz granulated sugar
175g/6oz dates, chopped

Combine the wine and vanilla pod in a large saucepan. Add the figs, apricots and raisins. Simmer for about 7 minutes. Add the cranberries and simmer for another 10 minutes until the fruit is tender. Stir in 150g/5oz of the sugar. Simmer to dissolve the sugar, taste and add more sugar if neccesary. Remove from the heat. Stir in the dates and all to cool to room temperature.

Cover the compôte and refrigerate for at least 1 day to allow the flavours to mellow.

ALL-BERRY RUMPOT

The concept of a rumpot is to combine equal amounts of the freshest fruit and sugar, cover the fruit with alcohol and allow it to steep in a dark spot. As the summer progresses, keep adding to the rumpot, layering more fresh berries, sugar and rum. Make sure the berries show no signs of mould or the whole pot will be in jeopardy! Serve with cream or vanilla ice cream.

About 350g/12oz each: strawberries
raspberries, blackberries, blueberries,
redcurrants

About 1.8kg/4 lb granulated sugar
About 2 bottles good-quality rum,
brandy or vodka

Choose a large glass or ceramic jar with a tight-fighting lid. Wash and dry it thoroughly – the dishwasher is a good choice.

Select only the freshest, sweetest berries available. Remember, you want to add different berries to the rumpot as the summer progresses. Carefully rinse and dry one type of berry at a time, removing stalks and seeds as necessary. Weigh the fruit and add it to the container. Sprinkle over an equal amount of granulated sugar and cover with the rum, brandy or vodka. If the fruit floats to the top, cover with a piece of parchment paper.

Fit the lid on tightly and place container in a dark spot. Steep for at least 3 weeks but continue to add more fruit, sugar and rum as fresh berries come into season. The rumpot should last for months if properly managed.

APPLE SAUCE

This apple sauce is on the chunky side but it can be passed through a fine-mesh nylon sieve or a food mill for a smoother sauce. Use the basic sauce for other recipes, but be sure to try the spiced version: it's rich and spicy! This recipes makes about 750g/1½lb.

1.25kg/2½lb firm, flavoursome apples
125ml/4fl oz water
1 tbsp lemon juice

Combine the ingredients in a heavy saucepan. Simmer for about 40 minutes, stirring frequently, until the apples are very soft. Allow to cool slightly before mashing or sieving if required. It can be served warm or chilled.

BROWN SUGAR-CINNAMON VARIATION:
50g/2oz soft brown sugar
½ tsp ground cinnamon

1 tsp vanilla extract
3 tbsp unsalted butter

After cooking the basic sauce, stir in these ingredients.

MELON COMPÔTE

Perfectly ripe fruit is the key to this light and refreshing dessert. Make sure to choose at least two different colours of melon – Charentais and honeydew are nice.

3 ripe melons
65ml/2½fl oz fresh lime juice

40g/1½oz granulated sugar
25g/1oz fresh mint leaves, thinly sliced

TO DECORATE:
Sprig of fresh mint

Remove and discard the inner seeds from the melons.

Using a large melon baller, cut balls from each of the melons. Toss these with the remaining ingredients.

Refrigerate the compôte for at least 4 hours before serving decorated with fresh mint.

Right: All-Berry Rumpot

POACHED PEACHES IN ZINFANDEL

This is the perfect recipe for those first peaches of the season that sometimes lack flavour. It also makes for an elegant presentation; just drizzle with syrup and garnish with a mint sprig.

1 litre/1¾ pints red zinfandel wine	4 sprigs fresh mint
150-200g/5-7oz granulated sugar	3 strips lemon rind, white pith removed
1 cinnamon stick, 7.5cm/3in long	6 peaches, firm but not rock hard

Combine all the ingredients, except the peaches, in a saucepan just big enough to hold the peaches in a single layer when they are required. Bring to the simmer, stirring to dissolve the sugar. Taste and add the sugar, if necessary.

Add the peaches and cover with a circle of parchment paper to keep the fruit down. Simmer for 15-20 minutes until the peaches are tender. Remove the pan from the heat and set aside for the peaches and poaching liquid to cool completely.

Before serving, remove the peaches from the poaching liquid. Bring the liquid to the boil and reduce until the flavour is concentrated. Serve at once and drizzle the hot liquid over the peaches, or set aside to cool and serve later.

PEAR DUMPLINGS

Easier than pie! Pastry is wrapped around ripe pears stuffed with toasted nuts. Child's play – but adult's delight!

50g/2oz walnuts, toasted and chopped	2 egg yolks, size 3
40g/1½oz soft brown sugar	1 tbsp double cream
3/4 tsp ground cinnamon	1 quantity Classic Pie and Tart Pastry
4 firm, ripe pears, peeled and cored from the bottom	(see page 58), unbaked

Preheat the oven to 190°C/375°F/Gas 5. Line a baking sheet with parchment paper.

Toss together the nuts, sugar and cinnamon and fill each pear with the mixture. Whisk together the egg yolks and cream and set aside.

Working with half of the dough at a time, roll it out on a lightly floured surface to a 3mm/⅛in thickness. Cut out four 15-20cm/6-8 inch squares, depending on the size of the pears. Working with one pear at a time, place it in the centre of a pastry square. Bring the pastry corners up to the top, brush them with the egg and cream mixture and press the seams to seal. The pears will look like a four-cornered hat. Transfer the pear to the prepared baking sheet. Repeat this process with the remaining pastry and pears.

Brush the dough with the remaining glaze and decorate the outside with leaves or stems cut out from any remaining pastry, brushing again with the glaze.

Bake the pears in the centre of the oven for about 40 minutes until the pastry is golden brown and the pears are tender if you test them with a skewer.

POACHED PEARS

Classic and traditional, this recipe is the basis for many desserts. The pears are also delicious served with Red Berry Sauce (see page 60).

600ml/1 pint water	1 vanilla pod, split
200g/7oz granulated sugar	4 firm ripe pears, peeled, cored and cut
2 strips lemon rind, all white pith removed	in half lengthways
2 strips orange rind, all white pith removed	

Combine all the ingredients, except the pears, in a saucepan just big enough to hold the pears in a single layer when they are required. Simmer, stirring, until the sugar is dissolved. Add the pear halves, cover with a round of baking parchment and simmer gently for 12-15 minutes until the pears are just tender.

Remove the pan from the heat and allow the pears to cool completely in the poaching liquid. Cover and refrigerate until ready to serve.

STEWED RHUBARB WITH GRAPEFRUIT AND STRAWBERRIES

Rich and saucy, this dessert is surprising low in fat!

150g/5oz granulated sugar	225ml/8fl oz water
450g/1lb rhubarb, trimmed and cut into 2.5cm/1in chunks	350g/12oz strawberries, rinsed, hulled and quartered
1 sprig of rosemary	1 large grapefruit, peeled and sectioned
3 strips lemon rind	

Combine the sugar, rhubarb, rosemary, water and lemon rind in a large saucepan. Simmer for about 5 minutes, stirring frequently, until the rhubarb is just tender. Remove the saucepan from the heat and add the strawberries. Leave to cool to room temperature before gently stirring in the grapefruit sections. Cover and chill overnight.

Serve chilled or at room temperature.

Right: Poached Peaches in Zinfandel

BASICS

These are used throughout the book and are cross-referenced in their appropriate recipes. Be sure to read through the pastry tips on page 61 before you begin any pie or tart recipes, and happy baking!

GENOISE SPONGE

120g/4½oz plain flour
Pinch of salt
4 eggs, size 3

150g/5oz granulated sugar
¾ tsp vanilla essence
40g/1½oz unsalted butter, melted and cooled

Preheat the oven to 180°C/350°F/Gas 4. Grease and flour a 23cm/9in cake tin.

Sift the flour and the salt together. In a separate bowl, beat the eggs until foamy. Slowly add the sugar and continue beating until very thick and pale. Stir in the vanilla essence.

Using a large metal spoon, fold in the sifted flour, then gently fold in the butter. Pour the mixture into the prepared cake tin and smooth the surface. Bake it in the centre of the oven for 35-40 minutes until golden and the top springs back when touched.

Allow to cool for 5 minutes in the tin, then remove the sponge from the tin and invert on to a rack to cool completely.

GRAPEFRUIT CURD

A tasty alternative to the more traditional lemon curd, this makes a fabulous accompaniment to fresh berries, as well as the 'Grape-Fruit' Curd Tart (see page 20).

175ml/6fl oz grapefruit juice
4 egg yolks, size 3
100g/4oz granulated sugar

1 tbsp grated grapefruit rind
150g/5oz unsalted butter

Follow the instructions for making Lemon Curd (see above).

LEMON CURD

Use this tart and tasty curd as the filling for a summer tart, the basis of lemon mousse or in Raspberry-Lemon Mousse Cake (see page 42).

5 egg yolks, size 3
150g/5oz granulated sugar
120ml/4fl oz fresh lemon juice

1 tsp grated lemon rind
Pinch of salt

Combine all the ingredients in the top of a double boiler saucepan and place it over simmering water. (If you don't have a double boiler, use an ovenproof bowl placed over a saucepan of simmering water.) Stir the mixture often until it thickens, which should take about 15 minutes, or slightly longer if you aren't using a double boiler.

Remove the pan from the heat and allow the curd to cool a little before tranferring it to another bowl. Cover with clingfilm and refrigerate until cold.

PASTRY CREAM

This should make about 400ml/14fl oz.

325ml/11fl oz milk
4 egg yolks, size 3
65g/2½oz granulated sugar
2 tbsp cornflour

1 tsp vanilla essence
25g/1oz unsalted butter, softened and at room temperature

Bring the milk to the boil in a saucepan over medium-high heat. Meanwhile, in a bowl, whisk together the egg yolks, sugar and cornflour until well blended. Gradually whisk in the hot milk and then pour the mixture back into the pan.

Return the saucepan to a medium-low heat and stir constantly until the mixture is boiling and thickened.

Remove the pan from the heat and strain the mixture into a medium-sized bowl. Stir in the vanilla and butter and allow the pastry cream to cool for a little. Cover the bowl with clingfilm and refrigerate it until well chilled. Keep chilled and use within 3 days.

RECIPE INDEX

All-Berry Rumpot 52
almonds:
  Peach Almond Clafouti
    (variation) 32
  Plum-Almond Tart 26
apples:
  Apple Galette 18
  Apple Pear Pie 22
  Apple Sauce 52
  Apple Spice Cake 20
  Baked Apples 54
  Deep-dish Apple Crisp 20
  Pennsylvania Dutch Apple
    Torte 16
  Poached Apples with Apricots
    55
apricots:
  Apricot-Almond Tart
    (variation) 26
  Apricot Cheesecake 28
  Apricot Mousses 38
  Apricot Upside-down
    Gingerbread 16

apricots (dried):
  Poached Apples with Apricots
    55
  Winter Fruit Compôte 50

bananas:
  Banana-Rum Ice Cream 46
  Banana Waffles 34
berries:
  see also blackberries;
    raspberries, etc
  All-Berry Rumpot 52
  Berry Galette with Spice Crust
    16
  Berry Gratins 38
  Fruit Torte 28
  Red Berry Pudding 34
  Red Berry Sauce 60
blackberries:
  Blackberry-Rhubarb Pie 26
  Blackberry-White Chocolate
    Parfaits 42
  Individual Blackberry Summer
    Puddings 36
blackcurrants:
  Blackcurrant Granita 44
  Blackcurrant Mousses 40
blueberries:
  Blueberry Cornbread 30
  Blueberry Pudding 32
  Blueberry Queen of Puddings
    36
Brandied Peaches in Filo Cups 55

cakes:
  Apple Spice Cake 20
  Blackcurrant Mousse Cake
    (variation) 40
  Chocolate Roll Cake with
    Strawberry Fool 22
  Fruit Torte 28
  Fruity Upside-down Cake 28
  Linzertorte 14
  Orange Sunshine Cake 18
  Raspberry-Chocolate Tile Cake
    14
  Raspberry-Lemon Mousse
    Cake 42
  Virginia Sponge Cake with
    Fresh Cherries 24
Charlotte, Pear 40

cheesecakes:
  Apricot Cheesecake 28
  Raspberry Cheesecake 20
cherries:
  Chocolate-Cherry Ice Cream
    48
  Classic Cherry Clafouti 32
  Virginia Sponge Cake with
    Fresh Cherries 24
cherries (dried):
  Rice Pudding with Dried
    Cherries 30
chocolate:
  Blackberry-White Chocolate
    Parfaits 42
  Chocolate-Cherry Ice Cream
    48
  Chocolate Roll Cake with
    Strawberry Fool 22
  Chocolate Sabayon with Blood
    Oranges 38
  Chocolate Stuffed Pears 55
  Ganache Glaze 14
  Raspberry-Chocolate Tile Cake
    14
Choosing fruit, 9, 11
citrus:
  Citrus Crisp Cookies 32
  Citrus Terrine 54
clafoutis:
  Classic Cherry Clafouti 32
  Peach Almond Clafouti
    (variation) 32
Cobbler, Peach 34
Coconut Crème Caramels 41
compôtes:
  Melon Compôte 52
  Winter Fruit Compôte 50
Cookies, Citrus Crisp 32
Cornbread, Blueberry 30
cranberries:
  Apple Galette 18
  Cranberry-Pear Tart 18
  Cranberry Sorbet 46
cranberries (dried):
  Cranberry Scones 33
Cream, Ginger 33
Crème Brulée, Raspberry 41
Crème Caramel, Coconut 41
curd:
  Grapefruit Curd 58
  Lemon Curd 58

custards:
  Mrs Bell's Rhubarb Custard Pie
    26
  Passion Fruit Custards 40

dried fruit:
  Indian Puddings 36
  Winter Fruit Compote 50
Dumplings, Pear 56

figs (dried):
  Winter Fruit Compote 50
fools:
  Mango Fool 42
  Rhubarb Fool 41
  Strawberry Fool 38
Fruit Torte 28
Fruity Ice Cream 46
Fruity Upside-down Cake 28

galettes:
  Apple Galette 18
  Berry Galette with
    Spice Crust 16
  Galette Pastry 61
  Plum Galette 24
Ganache Glaze 14
Genoise Sponge 58
ginger:
  Apricot Upside-down
    Gingerbread 16
  Ginger Cream 33
granita:
  Blackcurrant Granita 44
  Mango Granita 46
'Grape-fruit' Curd Tart 20
grapefruit:
  Citrus Terrine 54
  Grapefruit Curd 58
  Pink Grapefruit Sorbet 48
  Stewed Rhubarb with
    Grapefruit and Strawberries
    56
grapes:
  'Grape-fruit' Curd Tart 20
Gratins, Berry 38

ice cream:
  Banana-Rum Ice Cream 46
  Chocolate-Cherry Ice Cream
    48
  Fruity Ice Cream 46

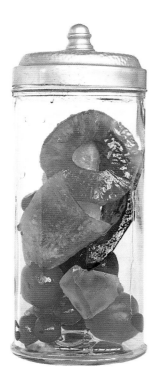

Lime Ice Cream 48
Nectarine-Cinnamon Ice
   Cream 46
Peach Ice Cream 44
Pina Colada Ice Cream 48
Strawberry Ice Cream 46
Vanilla Ice Cream 46
ices (water):
   see also sorbets
   Watermelon Ice 44
Indian Puddings 36

Key Lime Chiffon Pie 24
kiwi fruit 10

Lemon Curd:
   Lemon Curd Tart 28
   Mile-high Lemon Meringue Pie
      26
   Raspberry-Lemon Mousse
      Cake 42
lemons:
   Lemon Curd 58
   Lemon Sucker Sorbet 44
limes:
   Chilled Lime Sabayon 41
   Key Lime Chiffon Pie 24
   Lime Ice Cream 48
Linzertorte 14

mangoes:
   Mango Fool 42
   Mango Granita 46
   Mango-Raspberry Shortcakes
      33
melons:
   Melon Compôte 52
Mint-Orange Tea Sorbet 48
mousse cakes:
   Blackcurrant Mousse Cake
      (variation) 40
   Raspberry-Lemon Mousse
      Cake 42
mousses:
   Apricot Mousses 38
   Blackcurrant Mousses 40
Mrs Bell's Rhubarb Custard Pie 26
Muffins, Raspberry Drop 34

Nectarine-Cinnamon Ice Cream 46

oranges:
   Blood Orange Tart 22
   Chocolate Sabayon with Blood
      Oranges 38
   Citrus Terrine 54
   Mint-Orange Tea Sorbet 48

Orange Soufflé 42
Orange Sunshine Cake 18

papayas:
   Papaya Pineapple Salad 54
*Parfaits, Blackberry-White
   Chocolate 42*
passion fruit:
   Passion Fruit Custards 40
pastry:
   Classic Pie and Tart Pastry 61
   Galette Pastry 61
   Sweet Tart Pastry 60
   tips for making 61
Pastry Cream 58
peaches:
   Brandied Peaches in Filo Cups
      55
   Peach Almond Clafouti
      (variation) 32
   Peach Cobbler 34
   Peach Ice Cream 44
   Peach Melba Ice Cream
      (variation) 44
   Poached Peaches in Zinfandel
      56
pears:
   Apple Pear Pie 22
   Chocolate Stuffed Pears 55
   Cranberry-Pear Tart 18
   Pear Charlotte 40
   Pear Dumplings 56
   Pear Tart 22
   Poached Pears 56
   Poached Seckle Pears 50
   Shortcakes with Caramelized
      Pears and Ginger Cream 33
Pennsylvania Dutch Apple Torte 16
pies:
   Apple Pear Pie 22
   Blackberry-Rhubarb Pie 26
   Key Lime Chiffon Pie 24
   Mile-high Lemon Meringue Pie
      26
   Mrs Bell's Rhubarb Custard Pie
      26
Pina Colada Ice Cream 48
pineapples:
   Papaya Pineapple Salad 54
   Pina Colada Ice Cream 48
Pink Grapefruit Sorbet 48
plums:
   Plum-Almond Tart 26
   Plum Galette 24
   Plum Raspberry Sorbet 46
Pretzel Crust 60

puddings:
   Blueberry Pudding 32
   Blueberry Queen of Puddings,
      36
   Indian Puddings 36
   Individual Blackberry Summer
      Puddings 36
   Red Berry Pudding 34
   Rice Pudding with Dried
      Cherries 30

Queen of Puddings, Blueberry 36

raspberries:
   Berry Galette with Spice Crust
      16
   Linzertorte 14
   Mango-Raspberry Shortcakes
      33
   Peach Melba Ice Cream
      (variation) 44
   Plum Raspberry Sorbet 46
   Raspberry Cheesecake 20
   Raspberry-Chocolate Tile Cake
      14
   Raspberry Crème Brûlées 41
   Raspberry Drop
      Muffins 34
   Raspberry Ganache Tart 16
   Raspberry-Lemon Mousse
      Cake 42
Red Berry Pudding 34
Red Berry Sauce 60
Redcurrant Soufflé 38
rhubarb 11
   Berry Galette with Spice Crust
      16
   Blackberry-Rhubarb Pie 26
   Mrs Bell's Rhubarb Custard Pie
      26
   Rhubarb Fool 41
   Stewed Rhubarb with
      Grapefruit and Strawberries
      56
   Strawberry Shortcake with
      Rhubarb Fool 30
*Rice Pudding with Dried Cherries
   30*
Rumpot, All-Berry 52

sabayon:
   Chilled Lime Sabayon 41
   Chocolate Sabayon with Blood
      Oranges 38
sauces:
   Apple Sauce 52
   Red Berry Sauce 60

Scones, Cranberry 33
Shortcakes 60
   Mango-Raspberry Shortcakes
      33
   Shortcakes with Caramelized
      Pears and Ginger Cream 33
   Strawberry Shortcake with
      Rhubarb Fool 30
sorbets:
   Cranberry Sorbet 46
   Lemon Sucker Sorbet 44
   Mint-Orange Tea Sorbet 48
   Pink Grapefruit Sorbet 48
   Plum Raspberry Sorbet 46
soufflés:
   Orange Soufflé 42
   Redcurrant Soufflé 38
Sponge, Genoise 58
stone fruits 9
   Poached Stone Fruit 50
storecupboard 7
strawberries:
   Chocolate Roll Cake with
      Strawberry Fool 22
   Lemon Curd Tart 28
   Stewed Rhubarb with
      Grapefruit and Strawberries
      56
   Strawberry Fool 38
   Strawberry Ice Cream 46
   Strawberry Shortcake with
      Rhubarb Fool 30
*Summer Puddings, Individual
   Blackberry 36*
Sweet Tart Pastry 60

tarts:
   Blood Orange Tart 22
   Cranberry-Pear Tart 18
   'Grape-fruit' Curd Tart 20
   Pear Tart 22
   Pennsylvania Dutch Apple
      Torte 16
   Plum-Almond Tart 26
   Raspberry Ganache Tart 16
Terrine, Citrus 54

Vanilla Ice Cream 46
*Virginia Sponge Cake with Fresh
   Cherries 24*

Waffles, Banana 34
Watermelon Ice 44
Winter Fruit Compôte 50

ACKNOWLEDGEMENTS

I would like to thank my husband, Chris and my children, Alex and Tierney, for their patience and love during the busy time of preparing this book. They shared my excitement and enthusiasm for the project and kept the family going while I was cooking!

I would like to thank my terrific support team: the glue that held this writer's life together. Julie Fulop ran the house with confidence and love. Emily Head wrestled with the computer and won! Ann Mileti, Wendy Hyman and Jennifer Smith tested many, many recipes and offered their thoughtful insights to improve them. Many thanks to the staff at *Fine Cooking* Magazine, who graciously tolerated a slightly-distracted recipe tester. Kudos to my chief taste testers, Tim Johnson, Chris, Alex and Tierney Dodge, Ed and Ann Mileti, Andrew and Harriet Powell, and Mrs W. S. Mays; their refined palates and opinions were much appreciated.

Many thanks to my friend and food idol Martha Holmberg for bringing the project to me, and to Charlotte Umanoff, whose arrival gave me the time necessary to complete the task.

I would like to thank Grace Bell, Barbara Powell and Ann Mileti for contributing their delicious recipes. And, of course, my produce gurus, Nate and Hector at Hay Day in Westport, Connecticut for sharing their fruit wisdom and tolerating my endless questions and requests!

Last but not least, my deepest thanks to Laura Washburn, my editor at Weidenfeld & Nicolson, who led me through the maze of my first book. Robin Matthews for his sumptuous photographs, Roisin Nield for evoking a beautiful atmosphere and Emma Patmore, for creating the glorious food that brings the book to life!

Text copyright © Weidenfeld & Nicolson 1997

Photographs © Robin Matthews

First published in 1997 by

George Weidenfeld and Nicolson Limited

The Orion Publishing Group

Orion House

5 Upper St. Martin's Lane

London WC2H 9EA

British Library Cataloguing-in-Publication Data

A catalogue record for this book is available from the British Library.

ISBN 0-297-82214-4

Stylist: Roisin Nield

Home Economist: Emma Patmore

Designed by Paul Cooper